No Poster Boy

Trans Fag Essays

By Elliott DeLine

“The Borderlands” was originally appeared in *The New York Times* in May 2011. It was originally titled “Stuck at the Border Between the Sexes,” by *The New York Times* without the author’s consent.

“Stages of Visibility” was originally published in *Intertext*, the journal of the Syracuse University Writing Program, Spring 2012. The piece won the 2012 Louise Wetherbee Phelps Award for Writing.

“Dean and Teddy” was originally published in *Refuse,* as well as *The Collection: Short Fiction from the Transgender Vanguard.* Topside Press. 2012.

“Timid Boy Eating,” “Cisgender Gay Bullies,” and “The Trans Tribe and Grindr,” were originally published on OriginalPlumbing.com in 2012 and 2013.

“The Flesh Rampage,” was originally published in *Show Trans* , as well as TheAdvocate.com. 2014

“Trans People, Trauma, and Dissociative Identities,” “Dating While Trans: From Victim to Partner,” and “Being a Trans Guy and a Female Socialized Aspie,” were originally published on TheBodyIsNotAnApology.com, Summer 2015

“Self-Publishing as a Trans Person,” was originally published on TransGuys.com, October 2015

“Just Come in From the Rain” was originally published in *QED: A Journal in GLBTQ Worldmaking*, Michigan State University Press, October 2015

Underbelly Press
Syracuse, NY, USA

ElliottDeLine.com

IBSN: 978-0997216028

Cover photo of Elliott DeLine. Syracuse, New York.
Joseph Mudge © 2015

Contents

The
Borderlands 5

Stages of
Visibility...9

Dean &
Teddy..15

Gay
Bullies...29

The Flesh
Rampage...31

Timid Boy,
Eating...43

Like a
Flamingo..47

The Trans Tribe and Grindr..51

Sleeping with the
Enemy..55

Being a Trans Guy and a Female-Socialized Aspie..............63

Trans People, Trauma, and Dissociative Identities.............67

Dating While Trans: From Victim to Partner.....................73

Self-Publishing as a Trans Person......................................77

Just Come In From the Rain...81

The Borderlands

Some ignorant people assume transgender men are lesbians who couldn't handle being gay. They really think a female would go through all the hassles of transitioning to male just so she could trick other women into sleeping with her.

That just isn't the case at all, and as a transgender man, I find it highly offensive and presumptuous. They know nothing about me. I haven't gone through this to trick women. I much prefer tricking men.

Of course, that wasn't my intention when I started on testosterone as a sophomore in college. But all plans were uprooted when I left SUNY Purchase a year later because of an inconvenient major-depressive episode.

Since then, I've lived at home with my parents. I commute to Syracuse University but spend most of my time reading and writing in my bedroom. For about two years, I've lived a cerebral and celibate existence. As a pathological Morrissey fan, I find it suits me. Still, living in your childhood bedroom just isn't a sexy situation.

Not that my life was all that sexy before. I have been involved with a diverse array of people, but some key element was always missing. I've repeatedly found physical affection embarrassing and sex a wee bit soul crushing. Perhaps I expect too much. I just can't remember any experience that didn't induce more anxiety than it was worth. Relations with others seemed hopeless in this light.

Then I discovered a grimy gay bar and dance club in downtown Syracuse, one that attracts rowdy crowds and even has been featured in our local news for drunken brawls and stabbings. After spending so much time alone in bland, blue-collar, conservative suburbs, I gave up, gave in and attended a "college Thursday" hosted by a local drag queen.

I think I'm a fairly attractive guy. Therefore, walking into the joint, I actually felt sexy. I hated the music, the disco ball, the vibe, but I loved the attention. I was 22, but entering a room and feeling people's gazes was something I'd never experienced, at least not in a good way.

Drinking and talking with eager, mostly older gay men was immensely satisfying. One man bought me beer after beer and gave me $40 for (supposedly) no reason. It was exactly how I wanted it: a little scary, but mostly just a validating, homosocial environment. (Yes, I said "homosocial." Yes, I am a Humanities student.)

The free drinks caught up with me, though. Soon my reserved personality did a 180, and I found myself dancing in the sweaty crowd with my shirt off. My surgical scars were somewhat visible, but not enough that anyone in Syracuse would make anything of it.

In the haze, I received compliments, touches, kisses and several blatant offers that I politely refused. I whipped my shirt around like a flag and was even lifted up in the air by some big, macho dude while we made out. It was all quite lovely.

A few drinks and wretched pop songs later, I found myself hurrying to the parking lot with another young guy who told me I had "beer goggles" and that my dance partner was very unattractive. Thus, we should escape to his car. This was a guy I'd been eying all night, so I happily complied. I knew I'd have to explain eventually, but he was attractive, and I wanted to stall.

We made out in his car, but as things got progressively heated, I mumbled, "I have to tell you something."

He was surprised but didn't actually mind. For me, though, the fun was over. It wasn't long before I suggested we stop.

After that, going to the gay bar was less thrilling. I still felt people's gazes, but I couldn't help thinking they'd puke or laugh if they saw me naked. Melodramatic, I know, but my brain is a hyperbolic bully.

One night, drunk and depressed, I sat outside the bar with a shy lesbian who was willing to listen to my self-absorbed epiphanies.

"You see," I told her. "I assume gay men won't want me, so I'm shy and come off as snooty. It's a self-perpetuating cycle. In reality, I don't think I give men enough credit."

Another older woman joined us for a smoke. "Honey, why are you so sad?" she asked, tripping in her heels. "I'm going to find you a boy tonight."

"No, that's O.K."

"Come on. Why not?"

"I'm transgender," I said, drunk enough that I'd tell anyone willing to listen.

"Get out!" She paused. "Wait, explain what that means. I never go to gay bars. I'm new to this."

"I used to be a girl." I hate saying this, but it's the quickest way to communicate a complicated identity and process to someone new to the subject.

"No way!" she said, scrutinizing me. "I seriously would never know. You look legit."

"Yeah, I pass." Her enthusiasm didn't boost my confidence like I suspect she intended.

"So did you have the surgery?"

"Just my chest," I said. Obnoxiously, I lifted up my shirt, receiving a few oohs and wows of appreciation.

"So that's it then?"

Yes, nothing below the belt. I spared her why I thought that operation was impractical, not to mention unaffordable for me.

"And you want to be with a man?"

I hate being cornered. But once again, not wanting to get into a complicated, drunken discussion, I told her yes, that would be pleasant.

She stared off at the dark city streets, slightly slack-jawed, looking like her mind had just been blown to pieces. "Oh, honey," she said finally, "that's just so sad." She appeared to be genuinely moved by my plight and on the verge of tears. Then she said: "Wow, this is like super depressing. I have to go."

I can laugh about it now. Actually, I laughed pretty hard at the time. I know my love life doesn't have to be doomed. There are plenty of men and women who date trans men with no qualms. I don't even have to move to New York City or San Francisco — surprisingly, I've found several local guys who haven't cared.

But I never connect with any of them beyond a brief chat online and maybe (big maybe) a coffee date. I have no interest. I go home, freak out and block them from communicating with me so I don't have to think about it.

I wasn't always this jaded. I remember listening to that '90s song "Kiss Me" on the radio as a child. Love, I thought, should feel like that, full of slow dancing and moonlight and fireflies. Actually, I'd still go for that scenario.

I used to wish I were suave and casual, but I'm just not. Sober, I'm uptight. Drunk, I'm overwhelmed and whelming. So what do I want? I don't consider myself hip enough to be gay, and I don't desire a provincial, suburban life, either. I especially don't want children or to be married. Sometimes I daydream about having color-coded pets, and when one set died off, I'd get all new ones in a new color. I'd buy a moped and some suits, live in a Victorian house and go on long tropical vacations. But I never dream of a partner anymore.

The ideal of love got lost in the mess of analyzing gender and my own identity. It's a burden, having it take up my precious brain space. The nature-versus-nurture debate that most people leave in the classroom gnawed away at me for years as I tried to solve the unanswerable question of why I am what I am.

I think that's what my romp at the gay bar actually illuminated: I'm just sick of it. The angst, the guilt, the politics, the lingo, the whole transgender shebang: I want to put it behind me. But it's not really over, and maybe it never will be. Physically, I straddle the border of the sexes, whether I like it or not. I could try to celebrate my differences and pat my genderfluid self on the back for once.

But doing so would feel like lying to myself, and that's one trick I don't want to master.

Stages of Visibility

We were getting to know one another. I dread these classroom activities, but this one seemed to be going well. It was an LGBT Creative Nonfiction class, after all. This round, we were to tell a story of a journey we went on with someone we loved. I stalled and let Gina, the woman I was partnered with, go first. Then I decided to tell an emotional journey, rather than a literal journey. I was apprehensive—Gina's story led me to believe she was heterosexual and cisgender.

I told the story of my emotional rollercoaster with Isaac. I told her he already had a girlfriend, but was secretly involved with me. He would say he was going to break up with her, but it never happened, and he strung us both along for months.

Gina thought the story was really interesting, and was enthusiastic to hear more. Was Isaac bisexual, then?

I said, "Yeah, or gay in denial," and laughed.

The truth is, I just said that automatically. Really, Isaac and I are both transgender, and Isaac is queer and open to different types of people. I just found it easier to play the part of a regular gay man (whatever that means). I'm not sure if I was afraid she would judge me for being trans, or if I just wasn't in the mood to explain it. But why did I assume she would need an explanation? I guess, in my experience, most people don't know much about transgender men. I also have trouble talking about these things aloud, though I think I may want to and even need to. I was raised to be a very private person and to not make others uncomfortable.

*

In high school, I didn't like showering—I preferred just taking a bath so I could lie down. On my back, it didn't look or feel so bad, and submerged in hot water with my eyes closed, I could almost enjoy myself. But on mornings like this, when I was in a rush, I had to shower. I sometimes skipped days, but today I smelled weird so that wasn't an option.

I barely took note of my naked body—I washed it and my hair with soap then rinsed and was done with it. I scrubbed myself dry.

then wrapped the towel around my chest, wearing it like a dress. In the mirror, I looked at my head and shoulders and make-believed, just for a few seconds. Then I went back to my cold bedroom.

I had stolen about half of my brother's underwear. I was afraid to ask for my own—or worse, be seen shopping for them. This made my brother creeped out when he discovered me, but I kept doing it anyway. I pulled on a pair of small boxers, stretched and worn over the years, designed with a twelve-year-old boy in mind. Then I
slipped into baggy jeans, pulling them down below my hips—I'd read online that this would help me pass, as my ass would look flatter and young guys dressed in this manner. I searched for clean socks, then gave up and searched for the cleanest socks, pulling them each on as I stood on one foot.

My chest binder lay on the mattress where I'd left it. It was once white, but now a grayish yellow, with some green spots I suspected were algae, left from the few times I swam in the lake. It looked like (and was, for all practical purposes) a dingy tank top made of lycra. The only time I didn't wear it was when I showered. I'd tried it though. It was a battle getting into the thing. I took the neck hole and stretched it over my shoulders, usually burning them slightly in the process. I then wiggled it down to my stomach, and, putting my arms through the holes, pulled it up over my chest and back. I still feel revulsion recalling how I then reached inside my cleavage and spread my mammary glands apart, creating the appearance of a flat male chest.

I tried on various combinations of tee shirts and button-ups. I liked layers, to be safe, and I had read online that a white triangle of an undershirt beneath your collar gave off a masculine impression. After I settled on my usual army-green collared shirt, I looked in the mirror, parting my thick, still-wet, dark hair. Though cut short, it would be hours before it was dry. I made sure my bangs were swept off of my forehead— I had read, once again, online, that bangs were feminizing. I checked to make sure my hair around my ears was cropped enough— though I longed for sideburns, I couldn't grow them, and I was paranoid that allowing my hair there to grow long would make me look like Liza Minnelli.

After that, there was nothing else I could really do. I put on deodorant (unisex, as that was less scary to request my mom buy than men's). Before leaving I slipped on my skater sneakers (a few sizes too large, for effect) and added a third layer of a baggy hooded sweatshirt. I pushed out the door into the dark of the early April morning, backpack slung over one shoulder, hiding under my hood as I passed the other houses on the street and headed to the bus stop on the corner.

*

I was in homeroom, and, yet again, the teacher was doing roll call. "Laura DeLine?" It hurt to raise my hand. I was not this person anymore—I was Elliott. But there was nothing I could do. There would be a sheet in front of me. A test in French class. Name

___________.

I scribbled the first part so it was barely legible, then wrote DeLine. It felt like it was being beat into me for the millionth time. For the assignment, I had to write about myself. Je suis une fille.

I tried otherwise once and got an F. So I played along.

Square-dancing in gym class, we were split into boys and girls. Oh, how sorry I felt for the guy I was paired with. I said nothing. I bowed out early and skipped the class. I would not curtsy. There was only so much I could bear. I'd rather fail the class.

And nearly three years later, I emailed my college history professor. "If you don't mind, can you please change my name on the roster? I go by Elliott." In class, I had my notebook open, in the huge lecture hall. The professor was young but bald. He announced, "Oh, by the way, to anyone who emailed me asking to go by a different name...it's hard enough to learn all the students' real names. If you care so much, get it legally changed." Then he did roll call. I blushed and didn't say anything.

More years passed. I sat in another class—West African Literature and Politics. I was legally Elliott now. Roll call didn't hurt, I could write my preferred name on my papers. For homework, we had to read a disturbing story about female circumcision that made me wince with sympathy pains. So what do we think? Is it the West's place to interfere and stop this? My hand shot up immediately—I had meditated on this all week. "Let's hear from the women first," the professor said. I said nothing and lowered my hand. I spoke eventually from a distanced point of view with the other boys, never revealing that I cringed at the thought of my own clitoris being amputated and felt confused by the deep, empathetic connection I felt with these women, even if I didn't identify as female.

*

Class ended. Gina and I lagged behind as everyone else exited the room. "It's so funny," she said as she put her papers away. "I was the only one who noticed Jordan's the only straight guy in the class!" I nodded and smiled, unsure what to say.

"I couldn't be sure at first," she said, "but then you and Ian both said you were gay." I think she said this so I wouldn't be offended that she thought we were from the start.

"I'm not gay," I said, surprising myself a little. I realized it was very casual sounding, and that most guys would probably say something like, "I'm not gay! You thought I was gay?" Super defensive, even if they were open-minded. Gina must have noticed too, because she said, "Oh or queer or whatever."

"Yes, I am queer. Actually, I've had girlfriends," I said. "And it's kind of different for me, because I'm transgender. Female-to-male," I quickly added.

We'd packed up our books and laptops and headed into the hall. There were many students surrounding us, and I wondered if they could overhear us.

"So you used to be a woman?" I really don't look at it that way. "I was born female." I didn't like that either, but it seemed the quickest way to get her to understand.

"Seriously?" She didn't sound as shocked as I thought she would be. Still, it's clear she hadn't pegged me that way. I nodded, and we walked down the stairs. "Did you have the surgery?"

Invasive question. But I let things go sometimes. "I've had surgery on my chest," I said. I hate these moments. It seems like I can feel the other person trying to picture me naked.

"I would never know," Gina said. "Seriously. Never!" "Yep, I know." Should I have told her I don't need her approval? Told her that I wish I had the nerve, when cisgender people reassure me I'm handsome, to say "Really? I think you're hideous." As if I ever asked to be reassured... As if the subject were somehow up for debate... As if they were expressing some contrary opinion.

"I guess that's what you'd want though, right? Not to have anyone know?" She laughed, seeming a little nervous again.

I hate when people are too comfortable and therefore rude, but I hate when they are uncomfortable even more. So I smiled. "Well, honestly, it's a double-edged sword. I kinda feel invisible either way, it's---"

We were outside now. Gina avoided eye contact and didn't seem to be listening anymore. "---Never mind." I said.

"Well, see you later."

"Yep, bye!" I lowered my eyes and didn't see which direction she went. I walked across the quad, feeling the physical manifestations of anxiety—a sped up heartbeat, warm face, slight vertigo. But strangely, I also felt really good.

Dean and Teddy (A Short Story)

Colin and Dean arrived at the community center around dinnertime. "Go ahead without me," Colin said. "I have to use the bathroom." He turned down the corridor to his left. "It's the seventh door on the right," he added, gesturing towards the adjacent hall. "You can't miss it."

Dean stood alone, hesitant. He took several deep breaths as he walked down the hall, his wingtips tapping on the linoleum tiles. He could hear voices, but they sounded far away. He counted doors until he reached the seventh room. It sounded silent inside. Multi-colored flower leis and Mardi Gras beads trimmed the entranceway. A sticker on the door proclaimed it a "Safe Zone!" It didn't make him feel any better. Still, he turned the doorknob and stepped inside.

The room was small, with several bulletin boards and posters of smiling, same-sex couples nailed to the lime green walls. The back wall featured an amateur mural: a rainbow composed of multi-colored handprints with the word "ACCEPTANCE" painted beneath. Dean gave it a moody glance over the rim of his glasses. He took a seat in one of the orange plastic chairs, spreading his legs and slouching. There were three other people seated across from him, all sneaking looks in his direction. Feeling self-conscious, he sat up and crossed his legs. His right foot jiggled. He avoided eye contact.

In the circle there were, presumably, two other transgender men and one transgender woman. The woman wore a sack dress, a cardigan, and combat boots: all in black. Rings and bracelets covered her large, bony hands and her nails were speckled with chipping black nail polish. She hid behind the curtains of her dark hair, hunching her shoulders and resembling a large bat.

The boy to her right was wearing a tie-dyed tee shirt with cargo shorts. He had dirty, beaded dreadlocks and a patch of blonde fur growing on his chin. He was listening to his ipod, bowing his head gently with the beat. To his right sat a second boy. He was physically androgynous but had a macho style and general aura. His red hair was shaved military-style, his ears were gauged with black plugs, and there was a tattoo of a nautical star, among many freckles, on his left forearm. His tee shirt said, "Check a Box: Male, Female, Fuck You!" Naturally, there was a checkmark in the third box. He kept looking at Dean, and eventually crossed the room. "Hey man, what's good?" he asked, taking a seat beside him.

Dean scratched his left sideburn. "Oh. Hi. I don't know, nothing is especially good." He bared his teeth, attempting to smile, and lowered his head like an omega wolf.

The kid nodded. "Word, word. I'm TJ. 'sup."

Dean wasn't sure if *sup* was rhetorical. "Sup," he said, hoping, it functioned like *ça va* in French.

"What's your name, bro?" TJ asked.

"I'm Dean...comrade."

TJ didn't seem to pick up on the mockery. "Word, like Jimmy Dean! Cuz you're rockin' a pretty sweet pomp!"

"Excuse me?"

"Hair," TJ said, reaching out his small freckled hand.

"Yes. I have hair." Dean covered his head, flinching.

"I'm basically obsessed with James Dean," TJ said, putting his hands back in his pockets. "I base my philosophy for life off of him. Live fast and die young! I should get a tattoo of that next. I watched this movie about him once, it was epic. I think I was James Dean in another life."

Dean gave him a queasy smile.

"Hey TJ!" Colin had returned from the bathroom. He strutted across the room, his hands in the pockets of his zip-up sweatshirt. He had a slight frame and attractive, sharp facial features. His nose was especially prominent, though not bulbous. Dean always thought it gave him a majestic, bald eagle-like quality. He smiled as he approached, tossing his dark hair out of his eyes. He was very handsome, especially when he smiled.

"Colin!" TJ said. They slapped hands, clasping and releasing. Dean couldn't help but admire their synchronized, fraternal grace.

"How've you been, man!" Colin exclaimed. "It's been ages!"

"Tell me about it," said TJ. "Hey, nice shoes!"

Colin looked down at his white high-tops. The large tongues covered the ankles of his dark skinny jeans. "Oh, thanks! I like yours too. And your piercings, your hair, everything! You look awesome, dude."

TJ blushed. "*You* look awesome. The hormones sure did the trick. Made you really...manly, you know?" He blushed even redder, his face nearly matching his hair. "I mean, I don't mean that in a *gay* way."

Colin laughed, patting him on the back. "I know, I know. Thanks man. That means a lot."

Dean scowled, but no one noticed.

"So how's college?" TJ asked.

"Oh, you know, decent," Colin said. "How's high school?"

"Just finishing up. It's the shit, man."

Dean wondered if this was good or bad. He wished TJ would go away, forever.

"So you met Dean?" Colin said, placing his hand on his roommate's shoulder. Dean felt warmth spread through his body.

"Yeah! *James* Dean," said TJ. "I'm going to call him Jimmy."

"I'd rather you didn't," Dean muttered. His body was buzzing with warmth. He slipped off his black cardigan and rolled up his shirt sleeves.

"You even look like him!" TJ said, pointing at Dean's face. "When you came in, you were all brooding and shit. Blaze, doesn't this dude look like James Dean?"

The boy with the dreadlocks paused his ipod and gave Dean a look up and down. "Sort of," he said. "Actually, he looks more like...what's his name." He snapped his fingers repeatedly, his face scrunched up in thought.

"That's okay, don't bother." Dean mumbled. His heartbeat was racing. The more he tried to stop blushing, the hotter his cheeks burned. The girl in black was looking now as well.

"Robert Smith!" Blaze blurted. "That's the guy. You look like Robert Smith." He looked pleased with himself.

"No he doesn't," said the girl, not bothering to mask her disgust.

"Yes he does," Blaze said. "He looks just like him."

"No, he doesn't. Trust me, *I'd* know." She smirked. "You mean Morrissey. That's who he looks like. Sort of."

"No, I mean Robert Smith," Blaze said, "the guy from The

Smiths. You know, the flaming British guy, with the crazy hairdo. No offense, dude."

"None taken," Dean said, looking at his feet. His ears were ringing. *They're onto you,* said a cruel voice in his head. "But she's right." He pointed at the girl without looking up. "Robert Smith is from The Cure."

"Well same thing," said Blaze.

"*Not* the same thing," the girl said, narrowing her eyes.

Dean smiled at her. She looked confused and started cracking her bejeweled knuckles and chewing on a strand of her hair.

A fifth guy entered the room and closed the door behind him. "Alright, let's get started," he said, sitting down and crossing his legs. He was dressed in sportswear and looked like he'd come from the gym. His sneakers looked comical on his tiny feet. "Welcome to TransPride," he said, nodding around. "We are a support group for gender-variant youth, age fourteen to twenty-two." He smiled briefly, rubbing his goatee. "Go ahead and sign yourself in." He handed the clipboard to Blaze. "It looks like we've got some new faces tonight, so let's do a go-around. Everyone say your name, pronoun preference, a little introduction and um....your favorite candy." He cracked his knuckles and neck. "I'll start us off. Name's Ethan. I'm twenty-two. I identify as a straight trans man, and I prefer male pronouns. I'm a personal trainer. My favorite candy bar is Butterfingers." He nodded to Blaze. "Your turn, dude."

Blaze nodded stoically. "Hey. Blaze. Male-pronouns. I'm in high school. I play guitar. I'm an FTM. And yeah, Butterfingers are good."

"Thanks Blaze," Ethan said. "Teddy?"

The girl in black smiled halfheartedly. "Yeah, I'm Teddy. Female pronouns. If you feel the need to address me at all." She laughed, staring at the ground. "I'm trans....ish. And I dig Swedish Fish. I think. They're so much better in theory." She licked her lips, flicking lint off of her cardigan.

"Right," said Ethan. "Thanks Teddy. Next?"

Colin brushed his hair out of his eyes. "Hey, I'm Colin. I haven't been here in a few years, but I used to go as a teen. That was before I transitioned and all. But yeah. I'm twenty years old, and I'm a college student. I'm also in a band called Owl Eyes. I play guitar and write all the songs and stuff."

"No shit!" said Blaze, "For real?"

"Yeah," Colin said. "You've heard of us?"

"Everyone's heard of you," Teddy said.

TJ grinned. "I went to the shows *before* they were popular."

Colin smiled. "Yeah. You uh…sure did."

Dean smirked. He straightened up in his chair.

"Owl Eyes is sick, dude," Blaze said. "No lie, I've got you right here on my ipod."

"Awesome," Colin said. "Thanks guys. I'm glad you like us. But anyway, yeah. I identify as a trans guy. Male pronouns. And I really like Snickers. Especially the ice cream ones."

Dean felt his empty stomach rumble. Everyone turned towards him. He blushed, wondering if they had heard it. Then he realized it was his turn. "Oh," he said. "I'm Dean."

Everyone waited.

"I forgot the questions," he muttered.

"What did you say?" Ethan cupped a hand to his ear.

"He forgot the questions," Colin said.

"Oh," Ethan said. "Pronoun preference, identity, and favorite candy."

"Male pronouns," Dean said, sounding as if it were a shameful admission. He frowned for several seconds, staring at the mural. "I don't really like candy," he concluded.

TJ forced a skeptical cough. "You *don't* like *candy*?"

"I don't know," Dean said, adjusting his glasses. "Maybe. I like chocolate."

"That's candy!" TJ said.

"Okay."

There was silence again.

"Why don't you tell us about yourself?" Ethan said.

"I don't know," Dean said. "What do you mean?"

"Are you in college?"

"Yeah, he's my roommate," Colin said.

"What's your major?" Ethan asked.

"English," Dean said. "For now."

"And how do you identify?"

"I don't."

"Oh come on," Ethan said. "Of course you do! You're queer, right?"

"No."

TJ looked confused. "You're not? So you're straight? Wait, are you even trans?"

"Yeah, he's a trans guy," Colin said.

More silence.

"I have to go to the bathroom," Dean said.

"It's right down the hall," Colin said.

Dean sighed. "Never mind."

Silence again.

"Yeah. That's it," Dean mumbled.

Ethan nodded. "Okay, go ahead TJ."

"Okay," TJ said. "Sup. I'm TJ. I'm a radical queer, pre-t, straight-edge, vegan-anarchist trans guy. I prefer male pronouns, local music, and femme girls with tattoos." He grinned.

"Awesome," said Ethan, clapping his hands together. "Short and sweet. So, let's start the discussion by sharing two good and two bad things that happened this week. Colin and Dean, you're our guests tonight. Why don't you go first?"

The boys looked at each other. Dean shrugged passively.

Colin nodded. "Right. Well, I'll start off with the bad. I'm really stressed about final exams at school. And to make matters worse, I broke up with my girlfriend." He glanced to his right, but Dean was staring at the floor. "So that really sucked. But good news is, I got an email from this guy who wants to manage my band. It seems legit, and it's a great connection. He's well known in the industry, and that will save me a lot of stress. Other good news is...well, I've got my friend Dean here. It'll be nice to spend the weekend just hanging out at home. And I'm gonna take him to the ocean tonight."

Dean smiled, picking at his nails. He could hardly wait to get out of this place.

"Great!" Ethan said. "Thanks Colin. And what about you Dean?"

"Oh. Um, pass."

"No, no passing!" said TJ.

Dean scowled. "Well, okay. Um… I'll start with good things."

"Speak up!" Ethan said.

"I'll start with the good things," Dean said, not much louder. "I'm glad to get off campus with Colin. Yes. Also…I had a good breakfast."

"What was it?" TJ asked.

"A tangerine," Dean said.

"That's all?" TJ exclaimed.

"Yeah," Dean said.

"And the bad stuff?" Ethan said.

"Um…" Dean stared at the mural again, thinking. "I'm transgender, I guess. That's a bit of a hassle." He laughed. Teddy smirked but no one else reacted.

Ethan looked around the room. "Well thanks guys. Who wants to go next?"

"Me!" said TJ, quite literally on the edge of his plastic seat. "Bad: I had to work all weekend. Super lame. Also, I haven't been passing in public places, so that's bad for my ego. If you know what I mean. But good: I got my second tattoo." He pointed to the star on his arm. "And best of all, I finally start T in a week!" He was referring to testosterone injections.

"Congratulations!" Colin, Ethan, and Blaze said at different times. Dean nodded. Teddy didn't look up from her hands.

"Yeah I'm totally stoked," TJ said.

"Well good for you, buddy!" Ethan said. "You've been waiting so long." He turned to his left. "Your turn, Blaze."

"Nothing really happened," Blaze said. "I don't know. I got this new ipod." He showed it to everyone.

"Cool!" Ethan said. "That's alright, let us know if you think of anything else. Teddy, do you want to go next?" His voice was soft and he looked uneasy.

Teddy shrugged and sighed. "I don't mean to sound negative," she said, still looking down, "but nothing noteworthy *ever* happens to me. That's the thing. Maybe I can get some support. That's why we're here, right?" She snorted. TJ and Blaze shifted in their chairs, but Teddy continued. "I'll try to make it… brief. I know I've been criticized in the past for, um… ranting." She snorted again. "So anyway…here's my issue. Like many of you, I used to read transgender memoirs, almost obsessively. I'd sneak into the Gay section when my mom was at Barnes & Noble. I basically read them all. And every author says they feel like themselves once they transition, right? That they *finally see the woman in the mirror.*" She made quotation marks with her large, white fingers. "So I've dreamed of that day since I was a kid. And I don't regret my decision, but I'm telling you, I've been on estrogen for almost five years now. And when I look in the mirror, I still don't see the woman I want to see. The thing is, I can't see anything. My eyes look dead, my face is unexpressive... It's like I'm wearing a mask. It's almost more mysterious to me now then it was before. It's beyond freaky." She snorted again, but didn't smile. "Has anyone else experienced this?" She looked up, her pale cheeks tinged pink.

Ethan shook his head, staring down at the clipboard. Blaze was playing a game on his ipod. TJ was the first to speak. "I don't think that's normal," he said. "You should talk to a therapist-"

"Of course it's normal," Dean said, interrupting. Everyone turned, startled by his acerbic tone. He hesitated for second, scratching his head. "I mean, I feel that way," he muttered, "and I've been on testosterone for a while now."

Colin gave Dean a sideways glance. He was afraid where this was going.

Teddy pressed her palm to her forehead, grimacing. "But then what's the point?" she nearly yelled, her voice hoarse. "I was waiting for that shining moment, where I'd look in the mirror and finally see myself. I feel fucking cheated." She pounded her fist against her bare thigh.

Blaze and TJ made eye contact. "*Psycho,*" Blaze mouthed silently, raising his eyebrows.

"Yeah," Dean said, looking at Teddy's bowed head. "Yeah, that moment is a myth. I'm sorry."

TJ frowned. "I mean, not really…from what I hear-"

"So then what the hell am I doing?" Teddy said, ignoring TJ and looking into Dean's eyes. "Why the hell am I putting myself through all this shit? Years of therapy, invasive questions, electrolysis, voice lessons, tons of medical tests, losing my family and friends?"

"I can't answer that," Dean said quietly.

Teddy attacked her tears with the back of her hand. "I guess there is no point. I'm just sick." She smirked. "They were right about me. I don't know what I want."

"*No,*" Dean said, with surprising force. "No. You are *not* sick, and you *do* know what you want. You want to feel at home in your body, like anyone else."

"But I never will," Teddy said. "It's my brain that's fucked up, that's why. It's my attitude. My goddamn personality. Why can't I just be happy now, like everyone else? Why am I so ungrateful?"

"I agree with TJ," Ethan said. "This is something best left for therap-"

"Because to feel comfortable in your body, you can't think so much," Dean said. "And that goes for anyone, not just transgender people. But in order to get outside of your head, you need to take comfort in your body. It's like a Chinese finger trap. The more you struggle, the tighter its hold on you."

Teddy glared at him. "Don't give me any Zen bullshit," she said. "Trust me, I've heard it all." She nodded at the mural on the back wall. "Acceptance? Never." She laughed. "The day I accept *what God gave me* is the day I'm dead."

There were several moments of silence. Ethan cleared his throat. "Teddy, I'm sorry you're upset, but you know you can't say things like that here. There's a hotline you can call, listed on the bulletin board. But we really need to get on with our discussion."

Teddy gripped her hair with both hands. She didn't say anything.

"We're going to move on, okay?"

She nodded, not looking up. Her hair formed a curtain. She disappeared inside herself once more.

"Okay," Ethan said, pulling a stack of papers out from under his clipboard, "onto today's topic. I want to discuss the petition going around Facebook. Many of you have probably seen it, but in case you haven't, I'll explain. This Australian trans man was asked to take down shirtless photos of himself, because they were deemed *too graphic.* So the petition asks that all us guys pose shirtless in our profile picture, as a gesture of support. Transphobia will not be tolerated on the internet. It's time to show the world that we're real men, and they just have to deal with it."

"Word!" said TJ. "I'm totally down."

Colin nodded. "Yeah, I'd do that for sure. That's really fucked up of Facebook."

"I mean, to be fair, the Facebook staff apologized," Ethan said, "and they let the guy repost his photos. But I still think we need to make a point. Dean, Blaze, you in?

Blaze nodded. Dean didn't say anything. He was still looking at Teddy.

Colin shook his head at Ethan, making a slicing gesture across his neck.

"Oh," Ethan whispered loudly. "Right. Sorry I assumed. Well Dean, if you get surgery soon, you should really do it with us!"

Dean wasn't listening. "I'm not saying you shouldn't struggle," he said.

"What?" Ethan said.

Teddy looked up from her lap. "Then what are you saying?"

"Oh God, we're back on this?" Blaze said.

Ethan sighed. "We have several topics to cover tonight, so I'd appreciate it if we-"

"I'm saying you should keep struggling anyway." Dean said. "Maybe...I don't know...maybe you're getting closer. All I'm saying is, it's not as easy as waking up one morning and looking in a mirror. But so what? Who needs it? The whole transgender cult is stupid. What do they know about you or me?"

"Jesus Christ," Blaze said. "Let me know when this is over." He put his headphones back on.

Colin cringed. "Dean," he said, "you're getting really intense, man. This is how you offend people."

Dean looked into Colin's eyes. "I'm sorry," he said. "I'msorryI'msorry."

"It's alright," Colin said. "Just, like, think before you speak. You know?"

Dean felt his throat tighten. "I'm sorry." He folded his arms across his chest and hunched his shoulders.

"I mean, for some of us, it really is that simple," Ethan said. "I'm pleased with my reflection, and it's all thanks to testosterone. Granted, I don't stare. I'm not *vain.*" He laughed. "I'm a proud transgender man, and I'm proud to be queer. Is that wrong or something?"

"Maybe you guys need surgeries," TJ said. "It can do wonders. Sure helped me. There are lots of ways to earn the cash. My friend started a website so people could donate to him."

"Just takes a good old fashion work ethic," Ethan said. "If you want it enough, you'll find a way."

Teddy nodded to Dean. "Hey," she said softly. "Don't feel bad. I appreciate your honesty."

"I'm sorry," Dean said.

*

Colin stuck around for awhile after the group ended. TJ had discovered a new website for sex-toy reviews, and he wanted to share it with the other men. Dean felt awful, so he went outside for air.

The sun was setting and the lights in the parking lot were illuminated. The sky was streaked with orange and purple strati, and birds were singing their last songs of the evening. It was a cool evening in early May, and the air was still. Teddy was standing alone against the brick wall, hunched over in a leather jacket and sucking on a cigarette. Dean approached her, thinking that she resembled a cross between Patti Smith, Joey Ramone and a Halloween witch.

"I don't know why I bother," Teddy said before Dean could open his mouth to say hello. "I'm not like other transgender people. Those men all think I'm a crazy cat-lady before I even speak."

Dean sighed. "I'm sorry."

"Stop saying that!" Teddy said. "Look at me, kid."

Dean looked up at her. She was almost six feet tall, with heavy eyebrows and a sculpted, angry jaw. Her eyes were large and black, so the iris looked like two giant pupils. Her lips were raw and chapped, bloody red. "Don't ever be sorry," she said.

Dean could smell alcohol on her breath. He looked away, shy.

Teddy exhaled smoke, sighing. "Don't start thinking it's a guy thing, either. It's no different when trans women show up. Getting their hair done, facial reconstructions, breast implants...that's all they ever talk about. And sure, I'm a hypocrite. I mean, hey, I've changed my body with pills and what not. But I've never tried that hard to *be* anything. I just am. I'm not a real woman and I never will be. I don't want to be. Yet people look at me with pity because I don't pass and don't have the cash for surgery." She snorted. "Well, that's the best case scenario. This girl Jen posted about me on her blog, knowing I'd read it. She said I'm a *fetishist,* not a *real* trans woman. I mean, are you kidding me? What does that even mean? They think I masturbate in high heels or something? And so what if I did? What does that have to do with who I am?"

Dean said nothing. He was suddenly very tired.

Teddy ashed her cigarette with a violent flick. "It gets so you don't trust anybody," she said. "People who call themselves radical-sex-positive-queer-feminists still hold me up to this plastic ideal. They think I don't *know* I look like a guy in a wig? They think I haven't tried?" She laughed aggressively. "Well, I don't give a fuck anymore. I wasn't meant to blend in. If I cared about that, I wouldn't have transitioned in the first place. Half the time I wish I didn't. Back then I wasn't expected to belong to some stupid-ass community. At least back then I was invisible."

Dean stuck his hands in his jean pockets and leaned against the wall beside her. There were several centimeters between their shoulders, but he sensed her body seizing up. He sympathized, and took a step to his left. Looking at the sky, he said, "Oscar Wilde said that when the gods wish to punish us, they answer our prayers."

Teddy smirked. "That fat pedophile had an answer for everything, didn't he?"

"Sometimes I really think so."

Teddy smirked and blew smoke through her nostrils. "Listen Dean," she said, "you're alright. I don't use the internet anymore, and I definitely don't do phone calls. But take my home address." She unearthed a crumpled receipt and a pen from the deep pocket of her jumper and scribbled a few lines. "Write me sometime," she said, handing it to him. "I've always wanted a pen pal."

"I will," Dean said, folding the paper. "I definitely will. Thanks Teddy. You're pretty alright yourself."

Teddy took a silver flask out of her pocket. "If you say so, kid." She snorted, and took a big swig of liquor. As she wiped her mouth on her sleeve, she glanced down at the top of Dean's hair. It was dark and voluminous, much like hers, but because it was cropped, it stood straight up, leaving his face exposed. Still, one could get lost in such things...

Dean felt her stare, but he didn't mind. He wondered if she preferred The Cure or The Smiths, but couldn't bring himself to ask. He kept his head bowed, toying with the buttons on his cardigan. They stood still for several moments, listening to the birds in meditative silence.

Blaze and Ethan came out the door. Colin and TJ followed soon after, arm-in-arm and discussing testosterone injections. "You probably won't see changes for a few months," Colin said, "Except after a few weeks you'll get *a lot* hornier."

"Fuck yeah!" said TJ, pointing his left finger like a gun. "Look out ladies!"

Colin laughed. "Yeah, eventually you'll learn to control it. But for a while, you'll want to fuck every chick in sight." His eyes flicked towards Dean, as if daring him to speak. Dean didn't notice. He'd just seen a bat dart across the sky.

"Unless it makes me want dudes!" TJ said. "It can do that to some guys, did you know that? T turns them gay!" He laughed at the absurdity of it all.

Dean and Teddy met eyes, their expressions equally dour. Despite himself, Dean started to grin. Teddy couldn't help it. Behind her hair, she smiled as well.

Gay Bullies

Something I struggle with is accepting my genitalia. I don't believe I'll ever have surgery, and I've gone through several store-bought cocks, ranging in size, shape, and level of itchy discomfort, never feeling it did much for my self-esteem. Other people's comments have sometimes made things worse, particularly the comments of gay men.

My best friend in high school came out during our senior year of high school, and for whatever reason, he became something of a loathsome stereotype. His girl friends were suddenly his "bitches." He was constantly insulting every other gay guy we knew. And, aside from repeatedly telling everyone how well endowed he was, his favorite thing to talk about was his aversion to vaginas.

He had various reasons, always recited in the same, played-up manner for laughs. "Vaginas scare me! What if you get stuck inside?" Well, this was just as unlikely as getting stuck in an asshole. "They smell bad." Only if you don't bathe, and last I checked, the same applies to balls and assholes. "They're just weird." How can something that is on the bodies of half our population be weird? This same friend was more recently shocked to find out I had a date with a guy. "You mean a transgender one?" Nope, just your average gay. He couldn't believe it.

My freshmen year of college, a group of gay guys I briefly hung out with said similar things. It never did any good to call them out as offensive. The defense was always "How is it sexist? I'm gay! I can't help it if I don't like pussy!" Why is it anyway that our generation refers to genitalia in the singular form? Where, exactly, is the location of The Cock?

I've tried to tell guys such comments are hurtful, but this doesn't seem to work either. Another gay friend of mine would go on in his way about how he could "never date someone who bleeds all the time," and that he "was enough of a bitch on his own and didn't need to deal with someone's PMS." He'd talk about his dislike of feminine men ("Uh, if I wanted to date a girl, I wouldn't be gay"), masculine women, ("I hate when I see someone I think is a cute guy and then they turn out to be a lesbian! I feel tricked!") and vaginas ("I don't even know what they look like. That's how gay I am. I won't ever even look at one.") I had to say something.

"You do realize that as a trans guy, the things you're saying apply to me as well."

He missed the point. "Oh my god, I totally forget! I'm so sorry Ell, it's just, you look so good that I forget!" He added, "Really, it's a compliment."

I find myself making excuses for this kind of bullying behavior. Not everyone has been to college, learned trans 101, studied queer theory... But this is unfair to myself and other trans people. I've come to realize that understanding me isn't a matter of being an intellectual. Likewise, one doesn't have to be a radical to respect my feelings. Decent people consider how their comments affect others.

I don't think that anyone is good or bad in bed -- other people have argued with me, but I strongly believe it is a matter of chemistry and understanding between two people, and not an acquired skill. I've realized my attraction to people in the past had less to do with anatomy and more to do with a certain dynamic. It still is hurtful when people indirectly insult my body. But I try to think of it in terms of what James Dean said, about his sexuality: "Why would I want to go through life with one hand tied behind my back?" Such gay men have limited the people they will experience sexually. Even if this is what they prefer, by insulting us, they also lose out on a lot of potentially wonderful friends. In this sense, it truly is their loss, not ours.

The Flesh Rampage

I dragged Gabe to the local gay bar in downtown Syracuse. There was a triad of them: Trexx, Rain and Twist. Gabe hates bars, and so do I, but we had to do something, didn't we? We were both depressed beyond belief, stuck living with our parents, and besides, it was New Year's' Eve. At the time, Gabe was sleeping with some pudgy (allegedly smelly) kid whom he called Pasty.

"Why Pasty?" I had asked.

"Cuz the muthafucka's pasty!"

Gabe seemed to hate him. They had argued on the phone most of our drive. Pasty didn't like that his boyfriend was going out to a gay bar with another man on New Year's Eve. Gabe tried to explain that we were practically brothers, and had known one another since the eighth grade. But that only seemed to make matters worse.

"In a last ditch effort, I told him you're trans," Gabe said as we walked down the sidewalk, closing his phone.

"Why?" I asked, hiking up the collar of my black pea coat. In the winter, Gabe and I often matched, in our black pea coats, dark, slim-fit jeans, and black boots.

"I thought it would get him off my back. I'm sorry. You know I don't discriminate, but I figured it would shut him up for good."

I smirked. "Okay. I understand." Whatever.

Outside the bar, I saw a man waving. I didn't remember his name, but he always wore a baseball cap. He called me Harry Potter. Several of them do. That or Justin Beiber. I have a remarkable ability to morph into pop culture icons. He would assure me not all older men are creeps, rub my back, tell me I was a good kid for staying in school. He bought me Yuenglings, lit my cigarettes... He reminded me of an uncle I never had. A creepy uncle who was trying to get into my pants, but you take what you can get at times like this.

"Harry Potter!" Baseball Cap yelled, grinning, "So good to see you man!" He was dressed in a tuxedo, but still wearing that awful baseball cap. We embraced. I don't know why.

"Happy New Year," I said. "Nice suit." It really wasn't remarkable, but it seemed the appropriate thing to say.

"Thanks!"

"This is my friend Gabe."

Baseball Cap shook Gabe's hand but didn't really seem to care, because because Gabe is Filipino. Most men around here aren't "into" Asians. Baseball Cap looked perplexed for a second. Perhaps he expected Gabe's name to be Chang or something. He then moved his eyes back to my Irish features. There are no Filipinos in Harry Potter, as far as I know. No transsexuals either, but my pretend gay uncle didn't yet know that about me. Sure, I was too fem for a lot of gay guy's taste, but I didn't wear my main disclaimer on my face. Gabe sometimes resented me for that. I could feel it.

"Hey, come here," Baseball Cap said, putting his arm around my shoulder. "In case I don't see you again tonight, here's some cash." He pressed two twenties forcefully in my palm. "Have a great night, okay? Here's a pack of cigarettes too. Seriously, have a great night. You're young, you gotta enjoy it while you can. Dance, have fun, live a little for once! You deserve it."

"OK," I said. "Thanks."

"YOLO!"

"Right."

Gabe sighed as we walk away. "Be careful..."

"I am."

"Ew. He's pointing you out to people!"

"He is?"

"Yeah, to those drag queens."

I looked over my shoulder. I recognized one of the drag queens as someone I had once drunkenly told I was trans. She was black, stocky, shorter than the others, with a tight black dress and high heels. Her make-up and hair were less outrageous than the others. Maybe she was a trans woman. I wondered if she remembered I was transgender and if she would tell Baseball Cap. I didn't much care. It would make things more interesting. Who knows- sometimes it even made me more desirable.

I put the forty dollars in my wallet. Potency.

We entered Rain and sat down by the mirrors, beside an aging lesbian couple in cowboy hats. While Gabe went to the restroom, I thought about the two twenties burning hot in my wallet and admired my own reflection. The environment was too tame though. I had a small taste, and I was craving more.

*

We didn't last long at Rain. By eleven, we had smoked all Gabe's cigarettes, he was yawning and checking his phone, and so I drove him home. After I dropped him off, I decided to finally meet up with Michael. I parked my car in the lot off Westcott Street and walked to Taps—a real dive bar, hole-in-the-wall if I ever saw one. It was nondescript and one could easily overlook it. In fact, I had for months, but a Gabe had pointed it out a few days prior, saying, "Hey, did you know there was a bar there?"

In the entranceway, I showed my ID to a man on a barstool, hoping he wouldn't ask why it said I was female. "Mistake," I'd mumble, simultaneously ashamed of myself for being a freak and for being ashamed and considering myself a freak in the first place. The man didn't notice, or at least didn't comment.

I sat at the bar, out of place. A few patrons were punks, huddled at a table in the back, but most the people at the bar were blue-collar, non-descript white men, with one exception—a black guy, homeless or close to it from the looks of his clothes, was entertaining them loudly and wildly with a drunk story. The white men thundered with appreciative laughter. A football game was on the TV.

I ordered a pint of Guinness, and then another, gulping them at record speed due to nerves. I texted Michael under the table, telling him I was here. He said he'd be there any minute.

A few minutes later, I looked up from my Guinness and saw a tall black man's reflection in the mirror across from the bar. He had muscular arms— a linebacker's build— and I was instantly and strongly attracted to him. That's something rare for me to experience. He was wearing a t-shirt that said NAVY and the kind of sunglasses you'd expect someone to wear on a jetski. He wore the same glasses and shirt in the picture he had emailed me. It was definitely Michael.

I caught his eye and we both nodded. I spun around and stood up, shaking his hand jovially as if we were old pals. I could feel the other men looking at us—we were undoubtedly an odd pair. Michael stood about half a foot taller and was probably at least twice my weight. I couldn't hold his gaze for long, and only felt more anxious when he removed his sunglasses to reveal his dark eyes

He insisted on buying me another drink, so I sipped on a Corona with lime, despite that I'd reached my limit. We sat in the back, parallel to the punks.

Michael was (surprise) in the NAVY. Many men online said they were in the military—whether it's true I don't know. Syracuse is close to Fort Drum. He filled me in on all the missions and jargon and training. Having a change in heart, he was now going to nursing school. He wanted to save lives instead of ending them, he said.

It turned out he had previously been in a relationship with a trans woman, but never a trans man. I guess I misunderstood his response to my ad. He said wanted to experience it. It fascinated him. I drank faster.

"So what do you do?" Michael asked, changing the topic.

I said I worked at a library and was a writer. He laughed. "So you're like a librarian?"

"Yeah. Kind of."

"And what, you write like, magazines?"

"No, fictional things. Books."

He laughed again. "Like mysteries?"

"Not really." I started to explain but Michael cut me off to swear at the referee on television. Many of the men in the bar did the same. The punks glared at them.

Michael turned back, but didn't seem interested in continuing the conversation. He took off his hat and scratched his bald head. He then told a long, involved story about his time spent in Tijuana, pausing only to buy me a mix drink that I didn't ask for. "You have to gulp it fast!" It was red, white and blue and tasted like a popsicle.

"It was fun, but I don't recommend it," he said of Tijuana, "a man will get beat with a bat in the streets, and the cops will sit and watch. I've seen it happen. They just sit and watch."

I drove the car home on Michael's suggestion, despite how intoxicated I'd become. It was an extraordinary machine, with built in GPS navigation and satellite radio. I'd never driven a really nice car before, and was surprised how much fun I was having. We opened up the sunroof and cracked the windows. We cruised down the dark city streets, talking and enjoying ourselves.

Michael then asked if I was born female. Surprised by this, I responded yes. That had been in my ad... and I thought I had just explained.

"What surgeries did you have?" Well, that was in my ad too, but I explained my chest and the way testosterone injections masculinized my body.

"Well whatever you do works, because you're really cute," Michael said, groping my inner thigh. It made me blush.

"What is the rudest or most ignorant thing anyone ever asked you?" he asked.

"Um." I thought about it a second. "Well, I had a friend once in high school. I told him I was going to transition, and he asked if I would take pills and grow a penis. That was probably the stupidest question I've gotten."

Michael laughed. "I feel for you. When I was in 9th grade, I was literally the only black kid at my school in Cazenovia. Some kid asked me if black man sperm was the same as white man sperm. So I messed with him and told him mine was purple. And he believed me too." He laughed.

"Wow." I laughed harder than I would have sober. I was warming up to Michael. I wanted his hand back on my thigh. I found I often fell in love briefly and intensely while in moving vehicles.

We made out on his bed in the dark. My jeans were riding up on me unpleasantly. Drunk and free, I removed them, my tee shirt, and my underwear, grinning. Michael raised his eyebrows and grinned as well.

In my memory, there is a blank space here.

I sat on the toilet, naked, but nothing happened. I couldn't pee. Minutes passed and I began to sober up. I realized they weren't using a condom. I also realized I was really sore and wanted to go home. I headed back in the bedroom.

"Do you wanna ride me?" Michael was barely visible in the dark.

"I'm going home," I said.

"But I didn't make you cum..."

"Did you cum?"

"No."

Thank God. I pulled on my clothes.

Michael sighed and got dressed. "I'll drive you to your car."

*

"No one is available on Mondays," the receptionist said. She was a stout woman, with curly grey hair and glasses. Probably a volunteer.

"But you're called AIDS Community Resources..." I said, with obvious attitude, "there has to be someone I can see."

"Not til next week. And..." she checked a calendar, "All appointments look booked."

"Is there somewhere else I can go? A number I can call?"

"Well, they do STD testing at the County Health Center, but I don't know when. Here's the number."

She begrudgingly handed it over, avoiding the touch of my hand.

I sat in my car with my cell phone to my ear.

"Hello?"

"Hi there. ACR in Syracuse told me you could possibly give me a free STD test?"

"No, I'm sorry, those are only on Thursdays," the man said, "And we aren't doing them this week. We'll be at the ACR building in Syracuse next week to perform them."

"That's where I am now. They said they're booked next week."

"Oh. I'm sorry. Well, good luck to you sir. Try for the following week."

How in god's name was I supposed to wait that long? "Is there nowhere I can go? I'll travel if I have to."

"Well, there's Civic Center in Syracuse. They do free testing daily. Rapid Response tests are every Wednesday, noon to three."

I ended the call, annoyed. No one was going to tell me that?

I drove right down the road, less than a mile, to the Civic Center.

I walked up to a kiosk where a young woman was sifting through papers. She ignored me.

"Hi," I finally said, "Could you tell me–"

"You want room eight," she said, giving me a slightly disgusted look up and down.

"Excuse me? I–"

"STD testing, room eight," she said, gesturing at a pair of teenage girls laughing and chatting as they headed down the hall. "Follow them."

I sat in room eight, filling out the forms. I left my gender blank until the end. I eventually decided to make my own box. Next to it, I wrote "FTM" and put a check mark. I then returned the forms and received a number.

I sat in a blue plastic chair, avoiding eye contact with the mostly female occupants of the room, some with small children. The walls were covered in posters about abstinence. Tables were covered with pamphlets on every STD and drug under the sun, written in English and Spanish. I picked up one. "Do not have sex! It is the only sure way not to get Chlamydia." A cheesy, patronizing video—the kind one would watch in Health class—played in a loop on the television.

I texted Michael.

-Hey, we didn't use protection. You didn't finish, right?
-Nope. You?
-No. But I never do.
-That's really sad :-(
- You're sure you're clean right?
-Yeah, I got tested like a week ago.
-How long since you had sex before me?
-2 months, with my ex.

-Ok. But it takes 3 months to show up on a test...
-Trust me, I get checked all the time. I don't have HIV. I'm not some sort of asshole.
-Ok. But if you get a test soon, we can both know for sure.

I pressed send just as the nurse called my number.

"So I'll take a swab from the tip of your penis..." the nurse said, filling out a blue sheet of paper. We were seated in a small doctors' room. She was short, thin, probably in her mid fifties, but looked older.

I blushed. "Oh, I'm...well...Have you heard of transgender?"

The woman stared for a while before responding. "Yes?"

"Well I am that. Female-to-male. So I have a...vagina?"

She bit her lip, thinking. "So are you female or male?"

"Well, I...have a...vagina." Awkward pause. "I was born female."

"So you're a female." She rolled her eyes, ripping up the sheet and grabbing a new, pink one, with a drawing of ovaries and fallopian tubes. "From now on, save us time and put that on the sheet, otherwise we have to start all over. It said you were male."

"I put that I was FTM. That stands for female-to-male."

"Well, they crossed that out and checked male for you because of how you look."

"Oh."

"In that case, you'll need to get undressed."

Each crank hurt like hell. I'd learned to just dissociate in these kinds of situations. And when she scraped something deep with a large cue tip, the shooting pain brought back memories of the previous night. How bizarre, to hold this pose again so soon under such different circumstances. It made the sex seem invasive in retrospect.

"Alright, we'll have some results on Wednesday. Then it'll be another 3 months before HIV would show up."

"Thank you."

"And remember, put female on medical forms." She loomed over me like a threat. "Until you have a penis, you're a female. Got it?"

*

A few weeks later I was bored and on Craigslist again. Someone had posted an ad that caught my eye. "LOST CAUSE" it said. I clicked. There was a picture of Michael. The ad said:

BE CAREFUL THERE ARE GUYS ON HERE WHO WANNA GIVE PEOPLE HIV ON PURPOSE I SLEPT AROUND AND NOW I FOUND OUT I HAVE HIV I CAN'T SAY FOR FROM WHO BUT BE CAREFUL!!!

I emailed the anonymous address.

-Did we hook up? Is that your picture in the ad?
-No, but that's the guy who gave me HIV!!! he's sick and does it on purpose. HELP THE COMMUNITY, STOP NIGGERS FROM SPREADING DISEESE!!

I winced and closed out of the window. It seemed like a lie. It was probably a vengeful ex, or someone who'd been rejected, or just some psycho starting shit. I texted Michael.

-Um...did you see the post on Craigslist about you? You might wanna check it out...
-That's my ex. I'm suing him for libel yeah. Can you help me out and tell me the email address he's using? He's been hacking into my facebook too and telling my friends I have AIDS.
-OK. I believe you, but will you please come get tested with me? I don't know you.
-I don't believe this is bullshit. I really liked u and it takes something like this to get you to text me?
-I said it was a one time thing. I'm sorry, I had no idea you were hurt.
-Well I really like u
-Listen I wont know my HIV results til September. Can you go with me to the civic center just to get the rapid-result test? Just to ease my mind? Takes 10 min.

-I have work and school I cant just drop everything
-Please. anytime. Ill skip work if I have to.
-This is bullshit. I hate gay men. This is why I stuck with women for awhile, I dont need this drama.
-So you won't go?
- I got the test results right on my desk! I'm clean alright?
-Can I drive over and see it?
-I'm going away for work tonight.
-Can you text a pic?
-I really liked you. I hoped we'd have a regular thing maybe even something more. I cant believe you think that of me.
-I told you I wasn't looking for anything long term.
-Well I at least wanted to fuck you one more time. It was so good. You have a nice pussy.

My eyes welled up with tears. I could hear the word nice in my head, like frat boys over beers in some porno. "So I totally nailed her. She had such a tight pussy man. I destroyed that thing." "Nice."

-I don't care to hear that. Don't text again.

*

I kicked a pebble into the water. I watched as the circles spread outward like sonic waves and then disappeared.

Closing my eyes and inhaling through my nostrils, the lake air smelled like fish and algae. I removed all my garments, climbed up on the railing, and after a moment's hesitation, leapt into the dark water, feet first.

It was pleasantly cool—not a shock to my system but rejuvenation. I stayed submerged for several seconds, swimming near the rocky bottom. I spread my arms and open palms in a cyclical motion to propel forward. When I reached the sand bar, I came up for air, sputtering like humans always do.

I slicked back my hair and then ran my hands over my chest. It was largely numb, but that wasn't uncommon. My scars were a purplish white. It had only been a year since my surgery. What an ordeal. I still sometimes woke in a sweat, remembering the pain and the drug-induced panic. I knew I needed it, but I hadn't known how much it would change me. It was like an awakening. For the first in my life, I felt my body was sexually desirable. Such a realization was messing with my head. I didn't know how to store that knowledge.

My lower half was still submerged. I looked at it, glowing whitish green beneath the water. The rest wasn't visible to me without a mirror. It was only really seen by others.

"Nice."

I did a shallow dive and swam some more. Soon my mind went blank. I felt wonderfully alive and at peace, the way I imagine many people do making love. It was the first time I'd ever done this naked, and there seemed almost a symbolic, baptismal quality.

There was no one in sight, so I stood up in the shallows. I rested my hands on my glowing white ass and leaned my head back, looking up at the stars. The Syracuse pollution dimmed them, but out here in Cicero, further north of the city, it was a regular planetarium. I closed my eyes, content.

I resented the possibility of more doctors, medications, stigmas, and secrets. More questions of disclosure and reasons to be untouchable. An early death.

Yet there I was, knee deep in the lake water, smiling and wiggling my toes. I watched the mini, underwater sand storms stir up and then settle once more. I wasn't afraid. My body was something miraculous and self-healing, like a starfish. It wasn't teen-like impudence. I knew in my soul I would never wither.

I remembered our naked bodies pressed together. The rhythm. The strange and wonderful feeling of his entry, before the sobering pain.

Come what may. I regretted nothing.

Timid Boy, Eating

I can't remember the last time I ate something without adding up the calories in my head. As I write this, it is 11:30 AM. So far I have eaten two bowls of cereal, Greek yogurt a small portion of ravioli and some orange juice. I estimate that is around 800 calories. I mustn't eat any snacks, because I'll want to be able to eat dinner without guilt. What's bizarre is I am a very thin person, and always have been. I'm not sure why I do this.

When I went on testosterone, at age 20, I started feeling hungry all the time. It took me awhile to get used to a faster metabolism, and I gained about 20 pounds—still, I was an average weight. When I discovered this, I asked my parents if I looked fat—my mom told me I looked "husky." My dad said something about hormones making people bigger, and wasn't that what I wanted? "Careful what you wish for," his cruel tone implied.

I felt horrible. That was when I restricted my calories and exercised daily. It was an obsessive, but not all-together dangerous routine until I returned to school in the fall. I didn't know the calories in dining hall food and due to stress, began either binging and purging or not eating at all. I didn't tell anyone. A low point came when out for dinner with my kind-of boyfriend and his parents on his birthday, I spent twenty minutes in the bathroom, leaning over the toilet with my finger down my throat. I went back again to do the same after desert. When I returned, I was shaky and dazed and likely smelly. I could tell his parents were not impressed.

Since then I largely recovered, but I have to admit that such thoughts are starting to come back, nearly 2 years later. Though there is an abundance of information out there to help you cope with an eating disorder, rarely is there anything for men. At most, there is a disclaimer saying that it isn't unheard of, and mostly happens to gay men. Another generalization often made is that women become obsessed with looking thin and petite, whereas men focus on looking muscular. Never have I seen anything mention trans men, or trans women for that matter.

It makes sense to me. The cliché about eating disorders is that one does it to have a feeling of control, when their lives feel out of control. As a trans guy, my life and body felt foreign and unpredictable. I didn't want breasts, I couldn't predict the changes of hormones, and I began to have nightmares that I would become pregnant after sleeping with cis men. My calorie intake was one area where I thought I could take the reins.

Despite the fact that it was not geared towards me, I read all the literature I could about eating disorders. It was often difficult—it feels somewhat emasculating to even admit, as a guy, that you have an eating disorder. I fell pray to gender stereotypes and felt vain, weak, and womanly. It was doubly hard to read things as if I were a woman.

When I was struggling with this, I was afraid to tell people, particularly people who were heavier than me, out of fear that they'd take it personally. My best friend at the time was very fat and unhappy with it. When I told her I was anorexic, it caused a rift in our relationship. She took it personally.

I find people who insult fat people obnoxious and I get extremely annoyed by all the diet advertisements we are bombarded with on a daily basis. And yet, when it comes to my own body, I buy into it. Too much of my self-esteem is tangled up in being slim. I know that I'll never have the willpower to be a muscular guy, so I strive for a different ideal—the cute, skinny, hipster boy. An intellectual, emo twink.

I stumbled upon this character through my discovery of indie rock. When I was fifteen, I wanted more than anything to be magically transformed into Conor Oberst of Bright Eyes. Prior to going on hormones, I had a warped perception of myself as extremely curvaceous. I fantasized about being "angular." I wanted a chiseled, stubbly jaw line, a six-pack, boney elbows, hips that would fit in size 28 jeans, a thin face, and, above all else, a flat chest. I would see skinny artist or musician types and think, "That's me! That's what I should look like!

I was lucky: by physically transitioning, I ended up having a body that was close to my ideal. And yet, I'm still constantly worrying it could all go away at any moment—as if eating a second slice of pizza would turn me into someone grotesque and unrecognizable.

I wonder, is it common for trans people to have eating disorders? I've looked online for advice geared specifically to my demographic, but it's hard to even find help for men. I think, for me at least, there is a tremendous pressure to look good as a trans man. I know from experience that people look at you with a critical eye, to see how well you pass—I'm somewhat ashamed to admit that even I do it with other trans men, almost automatically. And it is also hard, even for me, to get rid of the prejudiced, automatic thought that a trans man who appears more physically, traditionally masculine is "more seriously trans" than those who are pre or non-everything.

So much of the trans narratives we regurgitate are about making our outside match our inside. I'm not saying this isn't what being transgender can feel like—but it certainly can lead to perfectionism. I sometimes have to stop myself and examine whether it's really my gender identity I'm trying to express, or some unattainable ideal. If too closely examined, it's almost impossible to tell. So much of becoming a sane person, for me, involves just learning to tune out thoughts. No more ruminating, planning, counting, or performing: just breathing, eating, living, and showing up. A little lack of self-awareness can be good for a person.

Like A Flamingo

I always hated the term transfag. I used to take real issue, first of all, with what I considered to be "made-up" words. I couldn't identify with a term that the average person in my town wouldn't understand. It seemed pretentious and useless. But as time has gone on, I've realized the average person actually understands very little about my life in general. It therefore would make sense that my identity was a "made-up" word. And really, the average person can deduce exactly what a trans fag is: a freak, and that's all they need to know. Trans, as in a tranny, the word they wrote in my yearbook. "Good luck with your sex change tranny!" Fag, as in a fucking faggot, rhymes with maggot, what they still yell at me as they speed by in their cars. How I hoped I could leave that behind in North Syracuse.

It's not a "reclaiming" of the term, so much as I just long for a noun sometimes. Just short little name for what I am. All these adjectives, ending with person. Well I don't feel like a person today. I feel like a crummy old fag. It took a long time to admit to myself that I don't hate labels — I just couldn't find one that fit. That's a scary place to be. But as I age, I find trans fag grows on me.

I do insist (or at least request) that when referring to me, you put a space between "trans" and any other word. It's always been an important matter of personal preference. When I see transman written as one word, I read it like I would Irishman or clansman. I suppose I am also a transman, but first and foremost, I am a *trans* man and a trans *man.* A trans man who loves other men, especially other trans men who love men. Now there's a mouthful. I am attracted to women sometimes as well, and I'm theoretically open to all genders. But being a man who loves a man is what really resonates with my soul, at least right now. That's why I don't understand people who ask, "Why didn't you just stay a woman then?"

First of all, I was never a woman. You could maybe make a case that I was a girl, but I started identifying as a trans guy at age sixteen, immediately after I learned that such things existed. I can't remember ever thinking of myself as woman. It's absurd. As feminine as I can sometimes be, I'd make a god-awful woman. Trust me.

It's like when people ask, "So you were born a woman?" Well, I didn't walk out of the womb with big tits and high-heels, if that's what you're asking. Not that these things a woman make. But no: I was not born a woman. I was born a baby, and I don't think I identified as anything except hungry and pissed off because I wanted to go back inside where it was safe and warm and people didn't constantly define me by how I looked. Well, that's not even true. They judged me via ultrasound. If I'd had a bigger penis/clit, they would have continued calling me Baby James and this whole ordeal could have been avoided. Still, some men are born with what the doctors designate a "micro-penis." Ouch, right? They have testicles and no vagina, but their penis isn't large enough to be distinguished from a large clitoris. Emphasis on the first syllable, by the way. Clit-or-is, not cli-tor-is. Shudder... So I figure that's what I have. A micro-penis, I mean. That's what it looks like. It's made of the same tissue, it's the same shape, and it's attached to a boy (me) so why can't it be? Truth is, I'm not all that hung up on it anymore. Back when I was, I wouldn't let myself look at it that way. I thought trans men who called it their cock were just kidding themselves. But now that I've come to peace with it, I can see that, hey, it kind of is a cock. Cool. I mean, it really is the same organ. One is just a bigger version with a urethra to ejaculate and piss. The other has no purpose other than to bring us pleasure.

But a micro-penis? God, that's horrible. Isn't there a different prefix we can use? Let's see... where's my thesaurus?
babyish, diminutive, dwarf, little, midget, mini , minute, petite, small, tiny, wee, bitsy, bitty, button, teensy, teensy-weensy, teeny, teeny-weeny, undersize, wee, weeny...

You get the idea. How about this? Let's judge everything with mine as the standard. Let's idealize small over big, like the Greeks. From now on, we can call what I have a penis — and aren't I lucky to be among the rare men who don't have one of those oversized ones? Yes, indeed.

But wait, then I'm just as bad as them. Nobody should feel ashamed of their genitals. And besides, I do like it when... never mind. Moving on.

The point is, I've decided mine works for me. I don't need to be secure in my masculinity, because I do not wish to be more masculine. I'm perfectly content with my gender, inside and out. No, I'll take it further — I'm perfectly content with who I am. My, how far I've come from the days I wrote *Refuse*!

Of course, I'm always hoping to grow. Pun intended. But it isn't a preoccupation.

What about... that, though? The other part? Well, why would I hate yet another thing only purpose is to give me pleasure? I mean, I personally don't have any other use for it. I've learned not to let the cultural and biological definitions infiltrate my confidence. It has nothing to do with babies or blood, which caused me so much anxiety over the years. Even if it did, whatever. I choose who and what I let in. It's simply a crevice. Like an armpit. Big deal.

Actually, I've come to rather enjoy it. I honestly don't know that I'd rather have a penis and testicles: I'm not a top, and I have my own method of getting testosterone, so why would I want to have something hanging down there, just waiting to get kicked? Why mess with a good thing? Even if there was a magic wand, I don't think I'd wish it were otherwise. I'd miss the feeling of what I've got. And I dare say I think that part of my body is sort of attractive. It took a long time to think this. Honestly, it dawned on me maybe a month ago, and who knows, maybe this good feeling will pass. The breasts had to go — my loathing was personal, instinctual, extending beyond the lessons society forced upon me. But this, I accept, and I think it's the real deal. It isn't emasculating, this sense of feminine masculinity — this desire to be fucked. Many men feel it. I've just got another option about how to go about it. It's just a personal preference. It isn't confusing, because it's my natural state.

Anyway, back to the term "trans fag." For me, being a trans fag is the recognition that you'll never be manly enough for society. You've embraced it instead of fighting it, the same way some cisgender men do. It's celebrating that you'll never be normal, and that in the eyes of many, your sexual desires undermine your identity as a man. Being a fag, especially a trans fag, means not giving a fuck.

Femininity once was thrust upon me. It meant self-denial, submission, and pain. Now, femininity is power, self-respect, honesty, and rebellion. It is being a man on my own terms, making me kinder, sexier, and happier than if I followed the rules. I can look at the color pink and say, "Hey, you know...it's actually kind of pretty, now that it isn't being shoved down my throat. Like a flamingo." Like a flamingo.

The Trans Tribe

I'm a little addicted to Grindr. I have never met anyone through this popular gay dating app, but I still am checking it constantly, using up all my data. I will be sipping coffee on the porch with my friend, nodding along to his story and thumbing my phone, as social convention now dictates as (almost) acceptable. "Do you think you'll get the job?" I'll ask him, while reading a yellow speech-bubble on a black page: So R U fully male?

I'll be in the car, chatting with my mom when I look down and read: Is it OK to ask if you still have a vagina? Have you always liked men? Have you always felt you were a man?

Even the well-meaning fellows send patronizing encouragements: Good for you! I am intrigued. You look great. You look so much like a guy. I'd never know you were a transgender. It takes courage to be who you really are. It must have been an incredible journey.

I could write an entire essay about my various tactics in responding. First, there was The Educator phase. Then there was The Doormat phase. Then there was The Rage, The Sarcasm, The What-Would-Oscar-Wilde-Say? Phase. I've settled into the Ignoring and Blocking Phase, often sending only a picture of the grumpy cat. "No. Just no."

Grindr recently underwent a makeover. Along with a few other new features, it now has "tribes." These are labels one can apply to oneself: Bear, Jock, Twink, etc. To check more than one you must pay money. You can now trim down your searches to the available subcultures, height, weight, body type, and race of your preference. You can also search for those who have checked the "Trans" box.

Much like would-be friendly liberal job applications that say "Male, female, transgender (circle one)," Grindr has completely missed the boat here. Under the trans tag you find a hodgepodge of trans men, trans women, crossdressers, daddies and meatheads who want to try something new. I was very confused when I started getting messages from men 600 miles away. How did you find me? I asked. Repeatedly, no reply. Then I figured out that they were searching for my tribe.

In response, I unchecked the trans tribe. My profile already says I'm trans, why would I want chasers from around the country hounding me? I already got enough shitty, stupid messages from my own area code. But then I started searching the tag myself, exhausted with the nonsense and hoping to just find some local trans guy and go out for coffee. Perhaps we could talk about something other than my body and identity. There were very few to be found within an 100 mile radius -- that is to say, few who kept that tag on their profile (and I can understand why).

I did start talking to a few guys who were far away, just making small talk. Soon we were sharing stories about the ridiculous things that were said to us. In the moment, and in my head, men's ignorant comments left me feeling dehumanized and vengeful. But talking to other trans guys, I could genuinely shake my head and laugh, the way I'd been trying to all along. I started getting messages from guys who didn't put they were trans, but were. And so unintentionally, Grindr had served to validate my experience and connect me, however briefly, to a handful other lonely trans guys with smart phones.

The realization was like a karate chop to my self-pity. When there were no "tribes" I could only see men in my less-than-glamorous upstate New York region. I was the only out trans guy that I had seen, and this was therefore (somewhat subconsciously) my perception of Grindr and even the gay male community at large: me, alone in a crowd of cis penises. Similarly, I wasn't getting that sort of support in my real life interactions. I know a lot of trans guys who live near me, most of whom are great, but none I'd been able to bond with over this issue. I brought it up at a discussion group once, and while people were sympathetic and supportive, no one had ever cruised cisgender men themselves. There was a sort of fascination with my tales, for cis and trans friends alike. Like, "I always heard rumors of the dreaded white, cisgender, middle-class gay male...but I never knew any trans man was so masochistic as to interact with one!"

The internet has been pivotal in the formation of modern transgender identities. While most dating sites -- scratch that, most websites in general -- do not accommodate us, and even invite hostility towards us, we have a secret weapon: hashtags. Tagging has helped us weed out a lot of crap to find one another -- to customize our experience of media, tailoring it to be affirming instead of degrading. We can't escape all of society's soul-crushing gender propaganda, but we can water it down, and we can share our ideas with others who share our values. I doubt I'd have any readership of my online writing or of my books if not for the #ftm hashtag. Though always applied with a little guilt, as if I am begging for attention, it has served me well again and again.

Throughout history, queer people have been able to survive because we are scavengers. We have scoured the antagonistic larger culture for anything useable, anything we could relate to or utilize to connect to others. In other words, we developed acute gaydar. We developed a camp aesthetic. Personally, I'm glad to be of a generation and locale that forced me to create my own queer icons without having them handed to me. This isn't to say I'd wish it on other people. Within the mainstream, straight-male-indie culture I was exposed to, I discovered The Smiths- - I was drawn to Morrissey like a magnet. Over a decade before J.K. Rowling announced that her character Professor Dumbledore was gay, I clung to the story of a misunderstood boy who lived in a closet in the suburbs, only to escape to a magical land one day on the motorcycle of a giant, hairy man who comes to his rescue, telling him he is not a nerd after all but a celebrity and a hero.

I never related much to transgender stuff -- books, movies, memoirs that were available, or at least known to me at the time. The internet gave me the bare bones of it all - instructions to follow, if you will - but it didn't give me the media and art that spoke to my longings. Nor did I know how to reach out to others, because the guys like me were the ones who read all the posts on the FTM Livejournal but were too shy to ever post. Consequently, we figured other trans men weren't like us. Now, us shy lads can just sneak in a #ftm and we're bound to get at least one "like." And sometimes that's all you need.

Tagging puts it all out in front of us at once. There will be a lot of stuff on #ftm or #trans* tags that I can't identify with. Stuff that may annoy the shit out of me. Searching #queer or #transgender, I may even come across bigotry and hate. But I also see that there are still decent people out there. And when I add tags to my posts or to my profiles, I attempt to give those people a way to find me. I can indulge in that silly dream all writers and romantics share - I can believe in a magical someone who completely understands and loves me, in a land of magical someones who completely understand and love me. And of course, they are only the best kind of someones: love and understanding means nothing here if it's not mutual. There's a spark of hope in an otherwise dim, dim, dim future of explaining to yet another anonymous torso picture that, No, I'm not a she-male. That's offensive, and more so than that, you're misunderstanding...Just forget it, I'm not interested.

I cling to my internet presence like a lotto ticket.

Sleeping with the Enemy

Today I came across a link on one of my newsfeeds. It was hidden among many other forceful, urgent messages and cat memes, but the headline caught me dead in my mindless-scrolling tracks: "Estimated 5 transgender people in the world killed a week." It's strange that after all these years, things like this never cease to shock me. Even after reading, it is unclear to me what is meant by "transgender people". I have no real sense of how many trans men, like myself, are victims of hate crimes. I have no idea statistically how high my risk is of being murdered- but anyone will tell you, not as high as someone like LaTeisha Green. She is a trans woman of color, murdered in 2008, whose killer is now going free. She was from Syracuse, my home, where I will return to tomorrow night. She wasn't the first, either. And God only knows all the unreported or misreported tragedies that have occurred in our little Rust Belt city. You don't have to look to history to find it - oppression is alive and well in "the Salt City," with its huge statue of Christopher Columbus in the center of downtown, its racially segregated ghettos surrounding the shining university on the hill, and its bland, isolated suburbs where people like me are bullied into normativity by (and I hate to stereotype but) Fox News-watching, Get-R-Done tee-shirt-wearing racist homophobes to the North, and Fox News-watching, would-be nouveau riche, equally racist homophobes to the East and West.

Upon returning home to a city that Bill O'Reilly once succinctly described on Fox News as, "NOT San Francisco," I do worry for my safety. I love Syracuse despite all of this, for all the good people who do live there. If I didn't love my city, I wouldn't dream of returning. And admittedly, I don't know how long I can stay. But I have plans to fight for the first time, and to involve myself in changing things. In some ways, it is for that reason I am more afraid than ever, for myself and my community. I often say I give Syracuse a *C-* for trans resources, and this is almost entirely due to the efforts of Syracuse trans people themselves. Smaller towns on the outskirts largely get *D*'s or *F*'s. Of course, there is no limit to how many minuses an *F* can get, when you're thinking globally. But anyway.

Reading the article about latest hate-crime statistics, I can't help wondering if some of those labeled lesbians over the years have been misgendered, and were actually transmasculine: binary or nonbinary. I know that if I had been murdered 5 years ago, it would have been classified as a woman, despite my identity or presentation. It's bizarre that regardless of gender identity, a male-assigned-at-birth person killed for dressing in "drag" is counted towards transgender murder statistics, as being under the "trans umbrella." But if a butch is killed, or a female in masculine dress, shouldn't that count as the same? For instance, look at the life of Leslie Feinberg, a person who was repeatedly targeted due to looking androgynous. If Leslie was killed, where would that crime have been marked down? While lesbian may not be *in*accurate in that hypothetical case, it's misleading, because someone looking at statistics will walk away with the sense that trans-masculine people are non-existent and/or privileged with safety. And while many of us have access to hormones and to passing, more of us, like myself, choose to live very openly. More of us are trying to establish ourselves as artists, writers, and distinguished members of our communities in general. Not all of those larger communities are accepting. I think it is therefore reasonable to always be prepared for the worst.

* * *

I am becoming more and more well known as a "transgender" in Syracuse. Even if I weren't a writer, people talk a lot of shit. I have overheard strangers in public discussing me and speculating, loudly, about my body, using my former name. The more confident I become, the more confrontational I become... and the more noticeable. I don't hide my identity. I've been featured in several publications at Syracuse University and within the community, as well as spoken at events and on the dreaded panels. I've even drunkenly outed myself into a microphone on stage at Trexx Nightclub... And then there's Google.

I decided from the start that as a writer, I was going to use my real name, even on the internet. I didn't really consider how damaging this could be until I lost my job at two libraries earlier this year. I can't prove it's because they found out I was trans. But the pieces fit. “You weren’t the person we thought you were,” I was told, vaguely. I had committed to transgressions and received no warning. Even publishing these blog entries is always a risk. Nowhere else have I talked as explicitly about my body and other topics that could be rationalized as deviant even (especially?) by HRC-loving liberals. Promoting my books is a risk. For this reason, I've never sought to get them in local libraries or to have events or publications mentioned in local newspapers. But several copies of *Refuse* did end up in the library system all on their own. The old edition. With my face on the cover.

While my passing/masculinity does protect me in some situations, I suspect that when people recognize me, it makes me even more freakish and threatening. At the same time, my pink button-down shirt, my crossed legs, the hummingbird brooch on my man purse, and the high-pitched noises I make about cats and puppies, also make me a visibly queer threat to some. After all, murderer Dwight DeLee shot LaTeisha Green because he didn't want any "faggots" around. Similarly, my best friend and I get this word shouted at us from cars. Recently, a check-out clerk at a garden center refused to speak to us, literally turning up her nose. We suspect it was because we were interpreted as an effeminate interracial gay couple, which wasn't too far off the mark. This was largely due to our appearance, but also because of our demonstrative excitement over statues of fat little sparrows wearing raincoats.

I think I am at the biggest risk when others find me sexually attractive. This is probably something I need to talk about in therapy, but hear me out. I've had pretty low self-esteem for a while now, particularly when it comes to my relationship with the queer, male, MSM community. On the other hand, transitioning (with chest surgery and all) made me feel somewhat desirable for the first time in...well, ever. I had a lot of pent up curiosities. I also spent a lot of time alone in my parents' house, unemployed, broke, and bored with a laptop. I can't be the only one who knows where this is going.

I gave up on Syracuse gays early. I didn't want to keep dealing with it, having to out myself (sometimes into a stolen drag queen's microphone) at some sleazy club, and having to watch someone weigh in his mind whether he could "get past" what was in my pants enough to take things further, physically or emotionally. I wrote in an old, published essay of mine that I hadn't personally experienced transphobia in the gay community. This was one of the stupidest things I've ever said. The questions and comments I repeatedly encountered were incredibly painful, discouraging, and bigoted.

On the internet I felt no differently. I had no desire to put myself out there as what felt like a defunct gay man – or worse, a gay impersonator. Messages I received confirmed my worst fears. Even those intended as compliments. ("Wow, you're hot and totally pass. All the other trans guys I've seen are gross." "Why would you bother transitioning if you want men?" "Did you have the surgery?" "You're saying no to ME? You don't even have a dick!" "I'll put my (blank) in (blank) but I'm not ever doing anything with your (blank). I'm way too gay for that.") Bi and even pansexuals were rarely any better, and they were few and far between. It was a numbers game, and I was also self-defeating. So I somehow found myself stumbling blindly into the world of straight men.

It was fairly simple. I just had to think how a bro would think, and put it in terms a bro would understand. I was driven largely by curiosity. The Syracuse University frat boys, the soldiers at Fort Drum, the cheating husband at the playground, all these macho types our society rewards - were they really as oblique as they appeared? Were they really as straight as they seemed? From what I can tell, it's the rare gay boy who hasn't fantasized about this – enough that a friend once expressed, and then retracted, that he was envious of my position. But in a way, I felt I had an "in" - I had something they wanted. As much as their praise was feminizing and made me feel like an object, I also, sadly, needed to hear it. I lean towards sub, bottom tendencies... so there is sometimes a thin line between feeling validated as a fem guy and feeling my gender identity is being disrespected. But at least I knew they were attracted to me. And when money got involved, it truly confirmed their desire. They weren't "getting past" it, like with gay men. There were less questions. And yet, they weren't getting "past" my masculinity either, because I think most of them had internal bisexual struggles going on. I think they found my body to be a safe outlet for that. This appealed to me. It seemed hot, in theory. In practice, not so much.

It became an addiction, in a very negative sense. When bored, I'd throw back a couple drinks and seek out risk on the internet and then in the world. I knew in the back of my mind that it was purposefully self-destructive. It was as if, just for a little while, I got to be someone other than me. I was casual, confident, emotionless - the only problem was, this isn't really who I am. When it came down to it, I was shy. I had trouble verbalizing what I wanted, let alone standing up for what I wanted. This included my desire to always use protection, which due to my inability to assert, landed me in several awkward visits to less than trans-friendly STD clinics. Even more difficult was expressing when I *didn't* want something, and standing up for my boundaries. This exacerbated past trauma, causing me to shut down further and blame myself, in a perpetual cycle. Later I'd be able to recognize I was raped during several encounters: but even now, it is hard to admit this and not blame myself.

It took me too long to realize I wasn't OK. The situations may have been playful fantasies in my mind, but all too often it was a sincere desire on the guy's' parts to degrade me, or at least elevate his sense of masculinity and phallic pride at my expense. Intellectually, I didn't feel degraded, but emotionally I found myself shaken and wondering why. As these "discreet" interactions continued, I found myself tolerating more and more bullshit. I've been hit with every transphobic question, statement, or slur, and usually, I'm ashamed to say, I've let them slide.

This is my theory: A cis man struggles to pin down what it is that makes someone like me attractive to him. To avoid being homosexual, he reduces me to my genitals, and perhaps emphasizes my size and stature. It's easier than ever, because cis straight men also reduce cis straight women in this manner. "Pussy is pussy." OK, fine. Sure. But I've grown more confident. I've decided I like my body and I like myself. Therefore, I started exuding confidence, and this is when cis men got scarier.

A man/boy who doesn't want a penis is hated. In my case I'm ambivalent. I do believe I have a penis, and well, whatever I have, I'm mostly fine with it at this point. But I found myself defending that identity/experience of "penislessness" to men who do have penises-defending my body as it stands, what they see as an irreconcilable pairing of traits. Deriving all their sexual self-esteem from their own dick, they don't want believe I can happily exist- they want to think I hate myself. People are sadistic. I don't mean to generalize about cis straight men. But I see patterns with the ones I've dealt with, not inherently because of their gender and sexuality, but from the fact that their privilege allows many of them to remain ignorant and foster a sense of entitlement and superiority. I think this character is especially prevalent in oppressed areas, and I'd venture to say it may even be a Syracuse thing.

Standing up for myself changed everything in my dynamic with my ex-cis "partners." Knowing that, I can't go back. I became conscious of the very real disrespect these men had towards me. I am consumed with a new kind of rage. Externalized rage. Productive rage. Confident rage.

The turning-point was a recent, passing incident - in the end it was only words that put me over the edge. It wasn't the time a guy choked me. It wasn't the time a man switched from my vagina to asshole without my consent. It wasn't the time I was told I should have stayed a girl because I'd probably look hotter, or the several times I was dubbed, as if it were the first time anyone ever thought of it, "the best of both worlds." It was two particular sentences that made me really fucking angry: *"I'm gonna fuck you like a little girl. I'm gonna make you take the dick you wish you had."*

Of course, this kind of verbal abuse had not been pre-established as OK. I didn't cry. I didn't feel bad about myself. Like someone reacting to a near death experience, I was calm and deliberate. I removed myself from the situation, then texted.

> "That was not OK. I won't tolerate being spoken to like that. I let some things slide in the past where many trans men would have kicked your ass. Not anymore. You don't get to say that shit to me. Don't contact me again."

* * *

I don't mean to project onto others, but I get so sad when I find myself perusing sites like Craigslist now, out of habit (funny/sad that unlike most dating/hookup sites, they actually have a trans section). I see mostly trans women posting in Syracuse, but increasingly trans men putting themselves out there as well, many in the same language I would use: language that I didn't want to use, and only tolerated for the sake of keeping painful conversations minimal. I'm sure there are plenty of people who have great experiences. Living in a more progressive city probably ups your chances of success - but it's certainly not a guarantee, as I've had equally awful interactions in Syracuse and the San FranCISco Bay Area (I am so punny). I know there are people who have no other choice, and people who feel empowered by casual sex and sex work. For some it's just a job. For others, it's just a way to get off. That's fine. I still get sad, because I think a lot of people are probably struggling like me deep down, and I hate to think about what happens and what will continue to happen. And it's perhaps a trope that homophobic men are actually homos... but I do think the "straight" or DL guys hooking up with trans people in secret are often dealing with some serious issues. They bring to mind ticking time bombs. The guy I was hooking up with revealed a lot in his words. "I'm going to *make* you..." I didn't like that. Not one bit. That might have been what I disliked the most. Nobody *makes* me do ANYTHING.

At my lowest point, I sat on a bench by the dirty creek in downtown Syracuse. As I lit a cigarette in the fading evening light, it occurred to me that I had become a statistic: though associated more with transfemininity than masculinity. I was transgender, fired, unemployed, enduring violence and abuse, secretly working in the underground market to save up and escape to San Francisco. Never had I felt more connected to my community and yet more alone.

* * *

I've often wanted to reach across boundaries and talk to trans women in Syracuse who post sex ads. Trans men too, but there's more weirdness involved there, as most of us know each other one way or another. Sometimes I dream that we "take back" the internet, posting clever messages of empowerment for one another and going on strike. No more fucking these men until they start joining us in the struggle. Maybe that's far-fetched, and maybe it's unfair. I don't even know that I'm really done forever. It's much like cigarettes. Gross cheap ones you don't even enjoy but keep smoking anyway. But at the very least, I think we've all gotta talk more about it: the way we interact with non-queer cis men. The mutual fetishization, fascination, shame, and hatred that too often accompanies this dynamic. And the danger, not just to our bodies but our collective sense of self-worth. At least I've got to talk about it. Heaven help me. I used to spend most of my time in my bedroom, writing, reading, and feeling sorry for myself. The past few years, that's changed. I've really put myself out there, as a "transgender," a writer, and a person. I'm learning what risks are worth taking. I will continue to speak my mind, to open people's eyes to what's happening in their own neighborhoods, right under their noses. I will continue to shoot off my mouth at men who sexually harass me online and in person. I never want to let anything slide ever again. They've got to realize we aren't taking this lying down. This means I've got to face my own sexual demons. I can't run from them anymore, shoving them in the bottom of my laundry bin or my sock drawer. I've got to articulate this to understand it, and understand it to accept myself, and accept myself before I can be of any help to anyone else who is struggling. And in this sense, my public introspection is political.

Being a Trans Guy and a Female Socialized Aspie

I have never been quite like most people. I was aware of my difference from a very early age. It was as though I viewed the world in an entirely different way from the people around me.

Things that they took seriously seemed inconsequential to me. Things that I took seriously seemed inconsequential to them. I felt perpetually misunderstood. Adults were always telling me I was "gifted" because I knew so much about animals, was a very fast learner, and could write and draw very well for my age. And yet, at the same time, it seemed as though I couldn't do anything right. I was always tripping over my own feet. I had trouble staying seated in school — literally. My body would slide out of the chair, and I would find myself on the floor. I couldn't stop daydreaming and looking out the window, no matter how hard I tried. I was petrified of talking to people.

"Little" things were big deals to me: my apple juice had to be just the right temperature, or I couldn't drink it. My blanket had to be cool to the touch for me to use it — but not too cool, either. I couldn't wear certain colors, such as yellow socks, because they were "itchy." I described many scenarios in everyday life as "uncomfortable." Shoes were uncomfortable. Going anywhere without a stuffed animal was uncomfortable. My parents were mostly amused by what they seemed to see as finickiness and bossiness. I would state my needs very clearly and not understand that they sounded bizarre to other people.

Adults also thought I was a liar because I often had extreme reactions to things, only to be fine the next moment. In school, I would report I had the worst headache and nausea of my life, only to find that it had suddenly disappeared when the teacher announced it was story time. These situations made me look dishonest, but I wasn't lying. Ailments would come with intensity and go away unexpectedly.

I also had a strong sense of justice and became overwhelmed with indignation and confusion when other people behaved cruelly. I remember doing so as early as my toddler years. I didn't understand other people at all. I didn't relate to girls, boys, or anyone, except animals.

Many trans people describe knowing that they were trans around age three. At around age three, I told my preschool teacher that I wanted to be a seal when I grew up.

Other quirks: I flapped my hands and arms when excited. I had trouble making eye contact. I zoned out and missed everything happening around me. I became fixated on one subject for long periods of time, to the point of obsession. And socializing was very difficult. I much preferred to live in my own world. These quirks carried on into adulthood.

It wasn't until last year, at the age of 24, that everything started making sense to me. I was a college grad, working a minimum-wage, part-time job at a coffee shop. And much like many other times in my life, I just wasn't getting it somehow. I accidentally burned myself regularly. I couldn't recall people's orders and would have to ask them to repeat them two, sometimes three times in a row. Despite knowing how, I couldn't count change and froze when someone gave me cash. People would ask me questions about the drinks and food, and I would be clueless. This wasn't the first time I'd struggled with a job. And yet, I knew I was intelligent. The amount of incompetence I felt was really bothering me.

One night after work, I talked to some of my newer friends about it. I expressed that I was afraid I was going to be fired. Not only was I unable to perform "simple" tasks, but I also couldn't seem to get the other workers to warm up to me. I didn't know what I was doing wrong. One of my friends, Joey — who is now my partner — said, "Well, it's hard when you're an Aspie." I had no idea what he was talking about. He then told me that he had Asperger's and that several people in our group of friends did. He was surprised I didn't realize I had it, too.

"Oh no," I said, thinking immediately of *Rain Man* or Sheldon Cooper from *The Big Bang Theory*. "I don't have Asperger's. I'm horrible with math and computer and science stuff."

I could see how Joey had Asperger's — and his son Drew, especially. They used to have a business in which they built remote-control planes. I had never met people as smart and as tech savvy — or as obsessive. They would have conversations in which I understood about two words, and Drew was only fourteen. Asperger's meant math/science super genius with no social skills, right? I was lacking in the latter — but also definitely lacking in the super-genius department. At least since my teen years, when math and science class started boring me.

Joey shook his head. "Do me a favor. Google search 'females with Asperger's,' or 'Aspie girls.' I know you don't identify as female, but you were raised that way." It's true. I'm transgender, and I was female assigned at birth.

And so I looked up female Aspies. I felt as though I were reading my own biography, even down to the detail of often not identifying with girls or gender at all. Others even had that difficulty with sitting in the chair. Everything I read described me perfectly. It was eerie. How had I never known this? I'd been sent to several specialists over the years. I'd been diagnosed with ADD, depression, and Borderline Personality Disorder — and yet, no one had ever suggested Asperger's. When I fit the description so perfectly, how had it gone undetected?

This weekend, I am at Flight Fest with Joey and Drew. It is a gathering of people interested in the building and flying of remote-control airplanes. I am not one of those people. It's interesting to be surrounded by so many people who are clearly Aspie and obsessed with planes. It makes me feel pretty neurotypical. And yet, I'm not. My obsessive areas of knowledge have been different from the stereotype, as they often are for female-socialized Aspies. I read a great quote once that explained why male-socialized Aspies stand out more. I'll paraphrase: An Aspie girl will be obsessed with horses. An Aspie boy will be obsessed with batteries. And for girls, the trouble socializing often goes undetected, because Aspie girls become obsessed with the study of interaction. They overcompensate, which makes sense given the emphasis of social graces for girls.

As far as the super-genius part: no, I have never been interested in how objects or concepts work if they don't relate back to people. My obsessions have ranged from animals, particularly cats, to Harry Potter, to the singer Morrissey of the 1980s British band The Smiths, to the works of the 19th century Russian author Dostoevsky, to the television show *King of the Hill*. There have been times in my life that I was pretty much only interested in things I could relate to these very specific topics. Recently, my interests have grown somewhat broader. I like social sciences, psychology, and different genres of music. But the amount of time I spent obsessively researching Morrissey, Drew spends researching planes and other stuff that I don't understand. I'm still an obsessive, prolific writer — and yet, I can barely do my laundry or remember to feed myself sometimes.

Of course, there are plenty of Aspies who don't fit the gender stereotypes. My partner was also female socialized, and he is much more mathematical and logical than I am. Some people have suggested a link between Asperger's and being transgender. I have definitely observed a link in myself and many people I've known. How much of this is biology? How much is socialization?

The truth is, I don't know. All I do know is that, when I looked up "Aspie girls," it was a huge relief to know I wasn't alone. I don't identify as female, but I identified with the stories I read. And now, I'm not as hard on myself for being different. All my life, I've been labeled as obsessive, weird, smart (but not "applying myself"), shy, lazy, awkward, gullible, and creepy.

But the truth is, I'm just Aspie. And I wouldn't want to "cure" that.

Trans People, Trauma, and Dissociative Identities

Many, if not most, of the trans people I've known have been coping with at least one form of trauma. We take a lot of abuse from society, often at an early age.

I am transgender. I do not currently identify as the sex I was assigned at birth (female). I have also taken physical steps to alter my body and live my life perceived by others as male. However, my gender identity is complicated, and it changes. The closest I can come to describing its current form is to say that I am a young, feminine male (no) boy (ugh!) boy-person. But there are parts of me that I identify as something different. This is partly because I have dissociative identities as a result of trauma.

Dissociative Identity Disorder (DID, formerly known as Multiple Personality Disorder, or MPD) is a highly controversial diagnosis for several reasons, and few people discuss it. In general, people want to believe that identity is immutable and stable. One body being inhabited by multiple people is not something that most folks can easily conceptualize. Plus, pop culture makes DID seem like a phenomenon that affects only extremely rare cases. No one really talks about what causes it, when the condition almost always serves the purpose of surviving repeated (often sexual) childhood trauma. Survivors generally are not believed about their perceptions. In fact, they often don't trust their own perceptions. Abusers depends on that.

I have sat witness to a many a conversation in which people — even trans people — have said that the only reason to disallow someone's transition is if they are "truly crazy — like schizophrenic or multiple personality disorders or something." This notion derives from the false belief that disabilities or mental differences render you incapable of consent and making decisions about your own body. You are seen as a danger to yourself, in need of protection from your own desires. But we "crazy" people still have the same rights as everyone else to self-determination.

And the truth is that most trans people are struggling with mental health. We just have to hide it or risk having our healthcare and agency taken away from us. And risk community shunning.

"You can't be a trans man and a drag queen," a local transgender leader informed the support group she was facilitating. "That doesn't exist.

And yet, I have been both these things, sometimes at once, sometimes separately. It's hard when your own community tells you that you don't exist.

Where I'm from, in order to start hormones, you need to do a "gender assessment." In my opinion, this is a form of conversion therapy. Essentially, a therapist goes down a checklist of gender stereotypes, and if you answer enough questions correctly, you get a letter saying you can transition to the "opposite gender." This process serves to weed out the "crazy" people and the ones who might "change their minds" — the people who only believe they are trans because of some gender-related trauma in their lives, or because they are trying to fool people, or because can't accept they are gay, or because of... whatever other anxiety cisgender people have about us controlling our own bodies.

By their standards, I probably should have been weeded out.

However, luckily for me, I passed the test. I was seventeen when I first started attending the Transgender Program at Goldberg Couple and Family Therapy Center (run by Syracuse University). I didn't have transportation. It took begging my mother and telling her I was just going to "talk things through." Eventually, she only took me because she hoped that I might work out my trans "problem" and be the normal girl she wanted.

This was not my plan, though. My plan was to start testosterone as soon as I could, because I was depressed out of my mind and hated my body and role in society. I didn't identify with my body. I was a boy. I had attempted suicide at fifteen, and I didn't want to go to that dark place again. I was saving myself, and it felt like the world was against me.

Even my therapist was a hurdle, not a source of therapy. In fact, the experience of therapy was traumatizing in itself. Non-binary expression was not allowed; in this sense, my therapy was the same as conversion therapy. My personal business was researched by university students. My sessions were videotaped for classroom sessions — something you had to agree to if you were to get their free services. As far as I knew, they were the only place to go in the area. As far as I knew, that was standard "transgender care" and the only way. And so I was a transgender guinea pig.

Questions I was asked: What do you think about when you masturbate? Do you imagine you ejaculate? Well that's sexual harassment, but I'm not going to call the therapist on it and risk not getting my letter. The truth was, I was usually dissociated while touching myself and didn't imagine much of anything. But yes, sure, let's say I imagine I am a male having heterosexual sex. That's the correct answer, right? One point for me.

Another question: Were you sexually abused as a child? Again, anyone else asking this out of the blue without getting to know me would be harassing me. But let's see... So they are trying to prove I have a clear bill of mental health, right? So was I sexually abused? No, I was in total denial at that point. That wasn't something that happened to people like me. I mean, sure, there were some disturbing, foggy memories...actually, many of them...But like my mom said, I had a very overactive imagination. I mean, that was the reason she thought I was saying I was a boy.

I fought her on that one, but in general, I doubted my own memories and perceptions. Plus, I was seventeen with no money and nowhere to go. I was pretty much stuck with my family of origin. You're asking me to face that my home may be an unsafe place for me? Not gonna happen. So no. Check mark, moving on.

Were you sexually abused or assaulted later in life? Well, again, that was only something that happened to ladies in dark alleys, so of course not. I wasn't going to face the fact that my first girlfriend — and the only thing close to a source of support from age 12 to 16 — was regularly raping me. Besides, boys can't get raped by girls, right? And she was younger than me...and I mean, I loved her. And I didn't exactly say no. Not every time. Let's not even bring that up. My answer is obviously no, I was never a lady attacked by a male rapist in a dark alley. Next question.

You see the problem. Therapy taught me that to be transgender, I had to solidify my denial. My trauma was buried even deeper. And that's when dissociative identities come out, because it all has to go somewhere.

So I want to do something I've never done before. I want to introduce you to Ellie. Most of my writing has been about Elliott, a male-ish identified trans person. In fact, Elliott is writing this now. But I'm going to let Ellie tell you a bit about herself.

*

Hi. I'm Ellie. I identify as a girl and transfeminine. I don't identify as a trans woman, because I was female assigned at birth, but I do relate to a lot of things about transfemininity because I live in a body that is usually interpreted as a male body, and I go by a male name and male pronouns most the time, even though it isn't my preference.

I identify as queer, but I'm pretty exclusively attracted to masculine men. Sometimes, I really wish Elliott didn't exist, because I want to be a girl and have people know it. I like being a girly girl...and I could easily just be a cis person and maybe even be good at it! I like being curvy, and I wish I had a more feminine figure.

Elliott and I had to make a deal that sometimes he will lower his testosterone when he is feeling safe about that, because it eases my anxiety. I want a booty, and testosterone ruins that! But I know having facial hair and being perceived as male is important to Elliott and both our identities are valid. It's really complicated and hard to work out. And we aren't even the only people in this body...

*

Seem far-fetched? Think I'm lying? Well, that's your choice. I thought I was lying at first, too. Sometimes I still think I am. But I'm not sure you really can lie about your sense of self.

OK, that was Elliott. Back to Ellie.

*

So I need to get dressed up sometimes in a girly way. I've only left the house a few times like this, but it's been very important to me. I also have struggled with sex addiction — getting drunk or high and meeting up with strangers. In fact, I became an amateur sex worker for a while, all on my own, with the help of Craigslist.

For a while, Elliott was in denial that I even existed, so it was easy for him to forget the things I would do. He could separate it from himself. See, that was the kind of thing Elliott would never do. It just doesn't fit at all with his personality. But when we started facing all the scary stuff that was happening, he started giving me, and the others, room to be ourselves. He stopped trying to control everything all the time. This happened because we got out of the old house and had space to be ourselves. We had support and met other people like us. It was kind of miraculous. But also hard work.

This doesn't mean that one of us is more valid than any other. And honestly, the hormone decisions are between us. The pressure put on us to be one, clear, cohesive, singularly gendered person is unfair. Human beings are complicated, and only we know what's best for our own bodies.

*

Phenomena like having DID and being transgender are not mutually exclusive. We are allowed to have intersecting identities. There are not real and fake trans people that need to be sifted out. Just because someone's experience differs from your own doesn't mean their need to control their body and their gender expression is any less urgent. So if we want to stop re-traumatizing trans people, particularly those who are non-binary, we need to let them have free access to hormones without psychiatrist gate-keepers.

Dating While Trans: From Victim to Partner

I've written quite extensively about my experience of dating cis people while trans — specifically, while being a female-assigned-at-birth boy, with a vulva, who is sexually and romantically attracted to men. I've tried on and tolerated several labels for who I am: gay trans man, trans fag, and during my more desperate, crude hours on online hookup ads, "Twinky, fem, bottom FTM boy with a pussy he was born with." It's a weird combination of speaking the language of the oppressors for their approval and giving a middle finger to the world by saying, "What's wrong with being that anyway?"

Reclamation? It's a messy business. Particularly when you are a sex worker, or have sex addiction and need a fix. Consequently, I ended up fucking with a lot of people who did not respect me.

I had two realms of "dating": strict hook-ups, sometimes for money, usually intoxicated and dissociated. And then regular dates, which were rarer, where a guy met me for dinner or coffee or something. The men of the first category were straight or bi and usually on the down low. They were often unstable and disrespectful. The men in the latter group were gay, bi, queer, pansexual cis boys who might have wanted to get to know me. They terrified and bored me. And often, they were equally offensive.

When I was in high school and my early 20s, I dated girls. That was when nobody else saw me as a boy. Once people did, my sexuality seemed to do a 180. My first real boy-crush was on a fellow trans guy in college. We never "dated," by his choice. We instead had a tragic *Brokeback Mountain*-esque affair; he had a girlfriend he was cheating on. When that ended, I was cured of my naïve illusion that two trans boys would be the perfect solution to all my angst. After that, I started with cis men, and similarly, it was usually a disaster.

After leaving college and coming back to Syracuse, I became pretty jaded by my repeated interactions with insensitive and clueless cisgender men. But my perspective has broadened. I now think about dating while trans in terms of how I treat others — in addition to how they treat me. I look at my own actions and don't just see myself as a victim of other people. I'm not saying that I haven't faced a lot of abuse. But currently, I'm more interested in writing about a new perspective, one that comes out of my year-and-a-half long serious, monogamous relationship with a trans man named Joey.

Suddenly, with Joey, the tables were turned. I found myself having to watch what I said and apologize for cissexist comments. As a trans person, I was not exempt. The pivotal moment for me came on our trip to Boston. It is hard to write about, because I do not come off looking good. But I feel it's important.

Drunk and messed up after giving a triggering reading at an open-mic, I said to my boyfriend, who I love dearly, that I wished he just had a big dick to fuck me, and that it was easy. It was a drunk, misguided attempt at flirtation, believe it or not.

I knew he wished this, too — and it wasn't exactly a secret that I was a bottom and physically enjoyed such things. Nevertheless, I shamed him for his body. And in the same night, I texted an old abusive cisgender ex to ask him "what was up." Luckily my phone died, and I confessed to Joey what I'd done. But this situation led to many big, difficult discussions and a lot of tears. We came pretty close to the end of what had been a great, loving relationship. I had admit to myself that I'd acted like a jerk. And I had to decide whether it was really Joey's body that I had a problem with, or whether it was the messages I had received about my own body and about what it means to be a real man.

I realized that it wasn't fair to put that on him. If I was going to love him, I had to love him for who he was, even the parts he didn't love. It wasn't my place to make matters worse. I had to get to know him and learn what language made him comfortable. Just because he didn't identify with his body didn't mean I could freely insult it. And so it took holding two seemingly opposing truths in my head at once: I love Joey, and his body, just as he is. And at the same time, his ideal image of his body is more sexually appealing to me.

But is it really just trans people who deal with this? The more I thought about society's influence on how we engage sexuality, I realized I didn't have an investment either way in Joey's body. I just wanted him to be comfortable. Whatever changes he made, I wanted it to be for himself. I realized my judgments weren't even my own, and that my perception of male beauty wasn't even my own. And actually, Joey is attractive to me — in the present tense. And that was why I wanted to date him. It was that simple.

As someone with Asperger's syndrome, I tend to be very blunt and honest and sometimes unaware of other people's feelings. Recently, I've realized that I've avoided looking at myself by always dating jerks. If I was the one being hurt, then I didn't have to worry about the responsibility for how I acted. But now, I'm with someone who treats me right. And, with few exceptions, I treat him right, too. But it was a hard fact for me to face that I have, on occasion, been abusive to him, even if I didn't mean to be. I'm not saying he's perfect, either. But this was my first real grown-up relationship. And it matters to me a lot. So I'm in therapy. I'm working on myself, because I want to be the sort of person who is a good partner. The oppression I've faced in my life has made it harder for me. But it's my job to fix it.

Sex is hard. Both of us are also survivors of repeated sexual abuse. We both carry a ton of baggage. We both have extreme body image issues. These issues are the hard part of our relationship as well as the source of its strength. We get each other. We support each other and can talk things through.

Dating while trans isn't just about other people discriminating against us. It's about learning to dismantle our own internalized discrimination and not inflict it on others. It's about treating others as you want to be treated. And I can see how it must have been for those people who dated me. Because honestly, it's not always easy to date trans people. We often have issues. It isn't our fault, but it's true. And personally, it's taken a lot of self-work for things to improve.

But all relationships take work. Isn't that what they say? I believe that Joey and I are both becoming stronger versions of ourselves by loving each other. So, for the first time, on this subject, I am not all doom and gloom. I am trans, and I have found love. But it wasn't easy, and it still isn't. It takes constantly checking in with myself to see whether I'm being treated okay, and it takes constantly checking in with myself to make sure I treat my partner okay, too. For me, it wasn't just hard to find love and trustworthiness in a partner. It was hard learning to how to love and be trustworthy as well.

Self-Publishing as a Trans Person

I love reading books. Particularly fiction and creative nonfiction. By creative nonfiction, I mean memoir that uses literary techniques. I also love writing both these genres. There is something that nonfiction books can't quite capture for me. There are feelings that are elicited from good storytelling, as opposed to just the basic facts. I love writing as an art form. To be cliché, it nourishes my soul.

I realized that female-to-male transgender people existed when I was sixteen. At that time, I was also an avid reader. I turned to the internet, and I found some books, but I was hard pressed to find art. Some things were helpful in telling me how people transitioned, what it cost (more than I could afford, I believed), and some useful terms. I bought a few books, and read the same stories each time: I was born this way, I came out later in life, I had the resources to transition. There wasn't much I could relate to as a poor—no, broke—young adult and burgeoning nonbinary (very) queer trans guy. This isn't to say there was nothing out there. But it certainly wasn't easily accessible for me, back in the 2000's in upstate New York.

I gave up on trans books pretty fast, and I found myself more drawn to books by other marginalized people, particularly from the 60's and 70's. I read literary classics by gay authors, black authors, female authors, indigenous authors, and authors at the intersections of these and other identities. The "firsts." I related to the oppression. I related to feeling like an outsider among outsiders. "Why," I thought, "is there no trans literature like this?!" Like I said, there were memoirs about transitions. There were nonfiction books. There were academic books. There were YA novels by cis people. But nothing that fed my mind and soul like these books I read by other marginalized people. Oh, and there was this one book I'd heard about, Stone Butch Blues ... but I didn't identify as butch. I identified as a fem, faggy trans guy actually. Little did I know how much that book would mean to me later on. But at the time, it seemed to be the only trans novel out there—and I resisted. I was not butch, and I was sick of people trying to point me in that direction.

I decided I had to write "the great American transgender novel." It was 2009 and I was 21 and pretty much a disaster in every area of my life. I wrote Refuse one summer, pouring my heart and soul (the good, the bad, and the ugly) into the pages.

It was a hot August evening when I finished, around the time of my 22nd birthday. It felt like I had finally done something important. I could feel its power. I knew it needed to be out in the world. I didn't realize how many others would relate ... In fact, I figured most trans people would hate it. But my story was burning to be told. I had to share my art or I was going to explode. I am not the most patient person ....

So now what? I had this manuscript. I edited it a million times. I needed someone to publish it for me, I thought. After several failed attempts to secure agents, get into fully-funded MFA programs, and even submitting the manuscript to several queer-focused publishing companies, I was pretty depressed. No one seemed interested.

But there was one person. The funny thing is, I don't even remember writing to him. His name is Mark Simpson, and he is the author of many books and articles about masculinity and gay culture and is actually the coiner of the term "metrosexual." But I personally knew of him because I had a well-read, dog-eared copy of his "psychobio" of my all-time favorite artist, the singer and lyricist Morrissey. It was titled *Saint Morrissey.* I must have reached out to several dozen trans authors. "Hey I have a book, can you read it? It's really different ... it's really good!" No responses. I don't remember exactly what it was I wrote to Mark. Some Morrissey reference. Something trying to be witty. Anyway, I heard back from him. And he said he wanted to read *Refuse.* And I nearly died.

A few weeks later, he told me he loved it and it needed to be published. And I actually did die that time.

He was a mentor to me at a time when I was a batshit crazy baby-author. He had good boundaries though. He didn't let me drool all over him. He was helpful and honest. He lived in England, so that helped keep some healthy distance as well. He tried to help me with a few connections, but we had no luck. Then he gave me the most salient advice would receive. "Why not just self-publish it?" He was an established author, and he was going to start switching to self-publishing himself, for financial reasons. This kind of just went over my head at first.

Because self-publishing is for failures! Oh how horrible that would be, to admit defeat. No, I actually wanted this book to be read (and make me money), not just sit on my personal bookshelf gaining dust while I slaved away at some minimum wage, transphobic job and lived with my parents. Refuse was supposed to change my life and launch my writing career. It was my only hope. Self-publishing was giving up, right?

I talked to my best friend about it. She poo-pooed self-publishing as well. But then I started having some thoughts. What if I embraced it? What if I used the internet to promote it, or just stuck flyers and stickers everywhere that trans readers might go? Did I really need anyone's permission? I might just be obsessive enough to pull this off, I thought. I had an image of it in my head ... I had long been inspired by punk and indie musicians. Why not treat literature like that? Who needed the gatekeepers? My friend at the time still turned up her nose, but I think it was because she was a little jealous of my vision, honestly.

And so I did it. And it worked. It wasn't overnight. But I self-promoted like crazy, bordering on spamming (a very delicate line, but just accept that you will cross it again and again and move on). With print-on-demand technology, it didn't cost me anything to publish. I started making some money. I started getting some reviews. I started getting haters. But most importantly, I got emails and messages from other fem, faggy trans guys that read something along the lines of "Holy crap, I thought I was the only person in the world like me. Did you read my thoughts and base this book off me or something?"

I think my book would have lost it's genuine quality if it had gone through professional editors and publishing companies and MFA critiques. I really do. I don't think it would have been as powerful. And now, 5 years and 2 books later, I do make a good chunk of the money I need to survive off of book sales. I don't think this would be the case, either, if I went with traditional publishing. Or waited.

So, if you are trans and you are bursting to tell your story, my advice is to self-publish. Start today. We're always waiting, aren't we? To get approval for hormones, to save up for surgery, to hear back from the doctor, to find someone-anyone- who understands us and wants to date us, for our parents to "come around," and tolerate us. I'm sick of all the waiting. Our lives are statistically shorter than most, so why add waiting for approval from more "experts" to that list? Artists don't need that. Believe in yourself and put your work out there. Make a blog, a zine, a self-published book ... it can be as cheap as you want it to be. Forget "aspiring." You're already a famous author. People just haven't discovered you yet.

Just Come in From the Rain

Let me begin by saying I am not an activist. I did consider myself to be one for approximately six months, from September 2013 to March 2014, during the time I was most active with the nonprofit I cofounded, CNY for Solidarity. CNY for Solidarity was an organization that provided vital resources and support to gender variant individuals and the LGBTQ community. We aimed to support the rights of all marginalized people in Syracuse, the surrounding area, and beyond. Our main focus was on those who are often overlooked by the larger LGBTQ community, with an emphasis on the intersectionality of classism, racism, sexism, homophobia, transphobia, and other forms of oppression. This article is, above all else, an exploration of why our organization fell apart.

My partner's teenage son told me the other day that I don't have enough opinions. He meant no harm by it, but I was hurt by his claim. He, like me, has Asperger's Syndrome, which means he isn't typically one for social graces. I admire his bluntness. In fact, I relate to it. My partner laughed. "No, Elliott has plenty of opinions. They get him in trouble, too."

But it takes someone being very close to me, or very distant, to know this. What do I mean? I mean that my partner and closest friends know me, as well as strangers who read my writing. Most people I interact with on a daily basis do not know my intensity, because I am programmed to be passive. Female socialization, anxiety disorders, a strong family history of alcoholism and abuse, internalized transgender oppression: there is a laundry list of theories as to why speaking up does not come naturally to me, outside of my writing.

Except when it does. It did with CNY for Solidarity. I do not have an answer book, but I do have some opinions in which I feel absolutely confident and for which I will fight. These are opinions that have to do with basic human rights. These opinions are anti-authoritarian. I have absolute conviction that transgender people deserve self-determination when it comes to how and when they make their transition. In other words, we deserve to have control over our own bodies. This is not the reality for most of us, and it is certainly not the case in Syracuse, where we are at the mercy of an outdated system of therapist and doctor gatekeepers associated with Syracuse University. This was one of CNY for Solidarity's greatest concerns and among the main reasons we formed the organization. To my shock, my conviction on this issue ultimately alienated me from most the powerful people in my local queer and trans community. This was because to challenge the status quo was to challenge all authority currently in place. And plenty of queer people had comfortable positions as a part of the oppressive system. African author Chinua Achebe wrote about such conditions in his description of the African elites who rose to power under Western colonialism in his novel *A Man of the People:*

"A man who has just come in from the rain and dried his body and put on dry clothes is more reluctant to go out again than another who has been indoors the whole time. The trouble . . . was that none of us had been indoors long enough to be able to say, to hell with it. We had all been in the rain together until yesterday."

Similar dynamics come into play with LGBTQ leaders with cushy careers in academia and nonprofit organizations. And Syracuse, as you may know, is a very rainy place.

Syracuse is a typical rustbelt city. That is to say it is a poor city. It is not an ideal place to be transgender: a population that is overwhelmingly poor. This is the typical narrative, and the path that I followed in 2005 when I was seventeen and grasping for resources that were all but impossible to find.

First, one Googles "Syracuse transgender resources" or something of the like. You will stumble upon a page created, and rarely updated, since the 1990s, that lists supposedly trans-friendly therapists and doctors in the area, who ultimately serve the more privileged, nonthreatening trans population "well enough." You will likely also stumble upon a social media page that is meant to serve as a local forum, but doesn't have much activity on it. My partner was a member of this online forum for several years before he learned there was an actual physical group that met up in Syracuse.

In 2007, I went away to college downstate, near New York City, where I finally was able to access the hormones I needed. After starting the transition, I came back to Syracuse because I was struggling with other mental-health issues and needed to move back in with my parents. In 2010, I enrolled at Syracuse University and finished up my English degree, but had little contact with other people. I was mostly a shut in. After graduating, unable to secure or keep a job, I spent several months in the San Francisco Bay area. But when my money ran out and my mental health got poor again, I returned to Syracuse. This time I was determined that if I had to live there, I was going to improve things. And I was going to start by making friends in the local trans community. After talking with new friends, it didn't take long for me to realize that not much had changed since 2005. People were still struggling to obtain health care as much as I did when I was seventeen.

Transgender lives are often not pretty. Many honest transgender narratives, therefore, are not pretty. Positioned as pariahs in society from an early age, our stories are often full of abuse, rape, bullying, self-doubt, and fractured experiences of our identities. They are tales of people living in survival mode. And yet to make the transition, we are expected to have a straightforward, non contradictory story of adequate mental health and certainty from an early age. This is a rarity among trans people—among all people. None of this should invalidate our current identities and the right to modify and control our bodies. Besides, it isn't just trans people who modify our bodies—it is an integral part of modern society. When a cisgender woman, for instance, wants breast augmentation, she is not required to undergo months, sometimes years, of psychological testing first. When a cisgender man is unhappy with the natural decrease of his sex drive and erections as he ages, he does not have to get a letter from a psychiatrist proving that it causes him significant enough angst to take medications. Only with what is perceived as cross-gender changes are such things required. This is due to social stigma, and not the consideration of patients' well-being (despite what we are told) and disregards our right to agency and autonomy.

When people need to make the transition and cannot, this often leads to depression and suicide. And it's just unfair.

I'd like to share the story of my experience with the Goldberg Couple and Family Therapy Center—the place trans people go in Syracuse to start their path to hormones. It is the place recommended on all local LGBTQ resource guides, and anyone at any local LGBTQ organization will point you there. Part of the appeal is that it's free. Another route could be trying to get a letter from a different therapist, but chances are they will be hesitant and costly.

I was sixteen when I knew I needed to make the transition to male. I was used as a guinea pig for Syracuse University psychology students. I was told that if I went through the "gender assessment program," I would get a letter allowing me to transition. I was subjected to inappropriate questions, such as what I thought about when I masturbated. Did I imagine I ejaculated? I was made to feel that if I answered these questions incorrectly, I would not be deemed "really male" and "really trans" or "stable enough" to transition. My body, mental health, and future were completely at the mercy of people who honestly knew less about transgender issues than I did.

The local support group I attended was little help—I was told this was just the way it was. There were various reasons I was delayed, and it wasn't until I went to a clinic in New York City in my twenties that I finally got the help I needed. The experience at Goldberg was traumatic and comparable to gay conversion therapy. In fact, gender assessments are a form of conversion therapy and should be treated as equally damaging. And when I found out years later, in 2014, that little had changed at this clinic, I was outraged. And I was even more shocked to find local support and activist groups had the same uncaring, complacent attitude.

When I learned that my friends were going through almost identical experiences in 2014, I wanted to create a forum to discuss all of this: that was the original purpose of CNY for Solidarity. At the same time, I learned that the murderer of LaTeisha Green, a local transgender woman, would be going free. Most community organizations seemed to be calling for overturning the decision, but I was more interested in addressing the issues that led to the murder in the first place. I felt both reactions were valid and necessary. I invited trans people to meet up at a local coffee house and discuss the questions, "What is working in Syracuse? What isn't? What would you like to see change? How can we work together to make that happen?" Out of these meetings, our grassroots movement was formed.

The mission of CNY for Solidarity was to empower people to control their own lives. We had several completely volunteer-run programs: an LGBT food pantry, a clothing drive, a support group with free meals, and various free clinics to educate people on their rights and available resources. The amount that we did with close to no money is shocking. The idea was to provide immediate relief. There was a disconnect for many over the degree of oppression most of the trans community faced. People did not have access to basic needs, like stable housing, healthcare, food, transportation, or safety from violence. CNY for Solidarity worked because it was run by the very people who were using the services. There was a sense of community, and of helping one another. This was a group to help the less visible transgender people, who were lacking community and were isolated from that community which did exist.

2014 services included, all volunteer-run, on a budget of about $1,000:

● LGBTQ Food Pantry: No ID required. Recommended for those with an income below $1,800 a month (for a single person). Fresh food available at Intersections meetings, and at other trans/LGBT social gatherings.
● The Free Bus to the Mazzoni Center.
● Trans Resources Packet (available online and distributed through the
community.
● The Intersections Café: Peer support and group discussions for LGBTQ
individuals plus a free meal and tea/coffee. This was a safe space to talk about how our sexual orientation and gender identities intersect with other struggles, such as racism, mental illness, poverty, homelessness, and more, with a big emphasis on respect and the

right to self-definition (things that we were not seeing at Transgender Alliance and other funded support groups in the area).

- Queer Mart: An LGBTQ Art and Craft Fair at the Westcott Community Center.
- Legal Name Change Workshops (with local lawyers, free).
- Group Shopping Trips (to thrift stores, for people who might be afraid to go into the men's/women's section alone).
- Trips to Safety First Syringe and Needle Exchange (because so many of us use needles for hormone injections . . . and they add up in cost).
- Individual Patient Advocacy for Doctor Appointments (to make sure people were treated with respect and were not abused, as trans people so often are).
- Workshops on Overcoming Obstacles to SNAP Benefits (because so many of us are need on them).

In the end, CNY for Solidarity was not welcomed and was delegitimized by the existing, funded LGB(t) organizations and leaders in the region. It was seemingly a threat to existing power structures. I couldn't figure it out at first. In the beginning, other local organizations, for the most part, were supportive of us. Then, as momentum picked up, it was as if we were suddenly blacklisted as radical rabble-rousers who were personally trying to start a "smear campaign" against the powers that be. This was spearheaded by a few powerful individuals in the Syracuse transgender community, older than myself, who I have been told called me a liar and said I needed to be silenced, because I was "alienating allies." CNY for Solidarity's mission was misinterpreted as a direct threat to their own power. I thought it was something that could be solved through conversation and explaining my intentions, but it seemed that the damage was done. These few people used their sway with other groups. No one wanted to rent us space. They didn't want to share our literature or events, despite requests. People told us they didn't want to "get in the middle." Board members began stepping down, fearing for their reputation and future working at other local (funded) nonprofits. It was a mess, but we were determined not to give up, and to keep our message positive: we weren't trying to dismiss and attack the work activists had already done in the past in Syracuse. But a lot more work needed to be done, and it hadn't been happening. We weren't out to point fingers, we just wanted to make change and help people to find resources. We tried desperately to collaborate and share ideas with other groups, but it became fruitless.

The biggest obstacle was our program called the Mazzoni Center Bus. The Mazzoni Center is an LGBTQ clinic in Philadelphia that provides trans-positive care. Let me explain the difference between trans-positive and trans-tolerant. Trans-tolerant is, at best, what is available in Syracuse. Trans-tolerant healthcare doesn't turn away trans patients, but it doesn't take us into account either. Our needs are "extra." Forms say "male or female," doctors are clueless and disrespectful, ask invasive, irrelevant questions about our bodies and spread misinformation. These doctors feel they are saviors, and they are taking a big risk by helping trans people and that we owe them unquestioning gratitude and compliance. They, as cisgender experts, know what's best. Again, you could try finding another, better physician, if you are privileged enough to have one, but good luck.

Trans-positive means we are welcomed and respected and accommodated, without having to constantly advocate for ourselves. In fact, the physicians advocate for you. At trans-positive clinics like the Mazzoni Center*, trans people are believed and respected enough to be given hormones without a lengthy assessment. They are given the facts, and they are respected to make their own decision for their bodies, without doctors interfering and deciding if they are "really transgender" or "really ready." It is interesting that this is the current recommended model by WPATH (World Professional Association for Transgender Health). Yet many people still see it as a radical, dangerous concept.

There was absolute denial that such trans-positive care was lacking and needed in Syracuse. Trans leaders in the community were insistent that Syracuse had an adequate system for making the transition and health care. People who reported abuse were singled out as liars or blamed or shunned as "not really trans" or "not ready to transition." I watched this happen again and again at the adult trans support group and the youth group at which I also volunteered. It was especially painful to see youth kept oblivious to existing resources out there, and therefore dependent and isolated.

Can I be honest? It hurts to write this. I've avoided it and put it off. It hurts because I believed so strongly in what we were doing, and it feels like we failed. It feels like we were betrayed by our own community. I still haven't worked out all the details of why the organization fell apart. I've come to view it as systemic denial, similar to the dynamics of an abusive family. CNY for Solidarity was a step towards admitting there was a problem. And the victims were blamed. Much like with my family of origin, I had to get away from the Syracuse transgender community to save myself. I didn't want people to have to go through what I did to make the transition and get health care. But the truth is, I'm still recovering from what has happened to me, and it is time for self-care.

Because we had less and less community support, barely anyone was showing up to our support group, no one knew about the food pantry, and we couldn't raise money to fund the Mazzoni Bus and other projects. I eventually stepped down as vice-president. Since then, CNY for Solidarity has been nothing but a Facebook group that people sometimes post articles on.

I have a major case of survivor's guilt. But I can't try to take on the entire system anymore. I have to put myself and my mental health first. All I can do is share my stories and hope that somehow makes a small difference. I still try to point people in the direction of resources when I can. But I don't obsess over it. I think, in the end, it will actually make me of better use to myself as well as others. To quote Audre Lorde, "Caring for myself is not self-indulgence, it is self-preservation, and that is an act of political warfare."

And that is why, at least for now, I am first and foremost a writer. I hope this article raises questions and starts discussions, and perhaps studies where trans people's voices are heard and they are appropriately compensated with money, so that these problems can be solved.

Recently I've been finding myself more interested in helping other trans people find the resources and tools to self-publish their writing, as I have. It may not seem as immediately pressing as a food pantry, health care, and relief like that. But I want to empower people to tell their stories, because it makes me feel more empowered too. People are often shocked to hear about the abuse that takes place, within our own communities, with therapists, in schools, and with doctors. Telling our stories is powerful. Trans people owning their perspectives and fighting to be heard are political acts that interest me. I recently set up a panel at a book fair in Washington, DC, called "Trans* Self-Publishers: Storytelling on Our Own Terms." It was meant to inspire and provide practical advice to others who want to write and self-publish. I've also started writing for an online magazine called The Body is Not an Apology about my struggles with loving myself and my body, and to tie my personal experiences to broader political issues. And hey, I managed to get through writing this article. I guess I can't really stop trying to fight for justice, despite myself. So maybe there's still some fight in me. And maybe one day I'll be able to consider myself an activist again.

*__Afternote__: I have since learned that the Mazzoni Center did not offer insurance that covers transgender surgeries for it's own employees as of 2015. This is extremely disappointing and hypocritical, particularly given that they hold *the* conference on transgender health care. Hopefully this mention will be a part of addressing and changing this injustice, if it hasn't already been remedied.

About the Author

Elliott DeLine (1988-) is the author of the novel *Refuse,* the novella *I Know Very Well How I Got My Name,* and the memoir *Show Trans.* In 2015, he was voted "Author of the Year" by readers of *FTM Magazine.* His essays and excerpts have been featured publications such as in *The New York Times, The Collection* from Topside Press, *Original Plumbing Magazine, QED, The Advocate,* and *The Body is Not an Apology.* In 2013- 2014, Elliott founded and was vice president of the non-profit CNY for Solidarity as well as the lead coordinator of Queer Mart, an LGBTQ artist and crafts fair in Syracuse, NY. In 2015-16, he lived for 9 months in a motorhome, traveling the USA with his partner Joey, Joey's son Drew, and their two cats Mittens and Snowflake. Elliott is also a visual artist, songwriter, friend to all animals, and an avid swimmer in all bodies of water.

Elliott is available to speak and read at colleges, community centers, events, and more! For more information, email elliottdeline@gmail.com or visit elliottdeline.com

Made in the USA
Middletown, DE
19 July 2016